GETTING
PAST
OK

GETTING PAST OK

A Straightforward Guide
To Having a Fantastic Life

Richard Brodie

∫∫∫ Integral Press
SEATTLE, WASHINGTON

© 1993 Richard Brodie
All rights reserved.

Published by Integral Press
1202 East Pike Street, Suite 786
Seattle, Washington 98122-3934
Tel: (206) 328-2217 · Fax: (206) 727-5130

Cover design: Rebecca Johnson

ISBN 0-9636001-0-9
Library of Congress Catalog Card Number: 93-77212

FIRST PRINTING, APRIL 1993

10 9 8 7 6 5 4 3 2 1

Manufactured in the United States of America

For Dana
who
upon opening a fortune cookie that predicted
"The current year will bring you much happiness"
replied
"I wish they'd be more specific."

♦

What's In It
For You?

P eople get *seriously* interested in improving the quality of their
lives in two situations: in The Pits, when things are so bad they
couldn't possibly get any worse, and just on the other side of The
Top of The World, when everything you thought would make you
happy has happened, and you're not. If you're *not* in either of these

situations—if things are more or less OK in your life right now—it may take a little prodding to motivate yourself to change; after all, things are, well, OK! Reading this book can help you discover that a life of enormous delight, passion, and satisfaction is waiting on the other side of OK, and can help you do what it takes to get there.

If you *are* in one of those two situations, you are already quite motivated to start making some changes, so I won't waste space trying to persuade you. I know. Not so long ago, I was in both situations simultaneously.

As one of Microsoft's early employees, I had struck it rich with stock options. I was the primary author of one of the world's best-selling computer programs, and was in charge of a secret new program with the potential to be even bigger. I had the money, the respect, even a bit of fame—a seven-second appearance on the *Today* show—yet inexplicably I felt worse than I ever had in my life. The stress got greater and greater, with no end in sight; finally, I felt I couldn't take any more. Seeing no other choice, I decided to end it all: I quit Microsoft.

I spent the next three years relaxing. It was a great luxury to have that option, and it did indeed remove most of the stress from my life, but it wasn't all that exciting either. I dabbled in various pursuits, met friends for lunch, and watched a lot of TV. Things didn't vary much from that routine until one day, comfortable but bored, I took the recommendation of a friend and went to a personal-growth seminar—and I only did it because he swore it would be fun and a good way to meet women!

At the seminar—which was fun, by the way, and a good way to meet women—I got a glimmer of something I had never consciously addressed before: the idea that there was something I could do to make my life more enjoyable and meaningful. At the time, this was just an intellectual idea; I didn't know what it would mean or feel like to have more fulfillment in my life. All I knew was that in the past, there had been times when I felt life was great, delightful, meaningful, worthwhile—and then, somehow, those times dissolved into the more usual texture of my life: coasting along, focusing on various problems or goals with a little boredom, a little anxiety, a little confusion, a little or a lot of stress. When I tried to get the good times back by attempting to repeat past experiences, it seldom worked, and when it did, the good times that resulted still filled only a short part of a long day.

But at this seminar, I got a glimmer of what was possible for me. I focused on the idea of figuring out what was most meaningful to me and getting more of it into my life. Having all the time in the world, I dove into the subject: I read books, took more seminars, beat drums, joined support groups, and investigated every method I heard about for improving my quality of life. Although I found a lot of whining, intellectualizing, evangelizing, and just plain con games, I found enough genuinely valuable material to keep me searching. There really was some good information out there, although in some cases it took work to find it and extricate it from the agenda of whatever organization was supplying it.

SUFFERING AND ENJOYING IT

Most of what I found, though, focused on how to handle crises; how to get through tough times. Much of the rest dealt with how to look at things in a different light, so the suffering really wasn't so bad. I wasn't interested in suffering and enjoying it! I was more interested in how I could make my life be about what I wanted it to be about—what I considered the most important, fulfilling use of my life—not on how to handle crisis after crisis, always putting off until later what I really wanted to do. I was not interested in enduring a lifetime of despair, waiting it out with the hope of retiring in my old age and going fishing. I didn't want my life to be about waiting!

Through lots of painful experience and trial and error, I found what I wanted: a legitimate body of knowledge I could—and did—use to transform my life from comfortable coasting to gut-satisfying fulfillment. I put together a set of tools that is thoroughly applicable to real people who have real jobs and real lives, not something for people with severe emotional problems, not something only for people who want an alternative lifestyle of meditating all day long or living in solitude in the woods, and certainly not something that involves swallowing a crock of pseudo-religious stew.

THIS BOOK

This book has three sections. The first section is about ways to understand as much as possible about what goes on in your life, on the theory that the more you know, the better equipped you are to make decisions. The second section is about ways to free yourself from the things in your life that drain your resources and prevent you from getting past OK. The third and most exciting section contains a step-by-step guide to discovering your own personal formula for success in life, a tool designed to take you past OK and help you keep the quality of your life well into the WOW zone.

Most of the ideas in this book are not original, but it took me a lot of work to find, filter, and organize them. I hope you will find the fruits of my labors useful in your own life. Who knows? Maybe someday having a fulfilling life will become commonplace.

This book is the happy result of years of frustration, amazement, and slow, painful learning in my attempt to improve the quality of my life. This is the book I wish had been written for me when I started my search. It's for people who, like me, want to have a meaningful life, not just survive until death.

If you are stuck in a rut, or unhappy in your life and are not quite sure how to change, this book is for you. If you feel powerless, controlled by others, unlucky, or desperate, this book is *really* for you.

But if you're like I was, pretty satisfied with your life, obviously doing well as far as other people can tell—if you're confident that you're a pretty good person and meet with most people's approval most of the time, and think that "personal growth" is something for gullible, weak-willed, or emotionally disturbed people—this book is *really, really, really* for you. You can have so much more. Take the time to read this and find out what you can do for yourself. If you put the information in this book into action, you will thank yourself every day for the rest of your life.

If you're already sold on the value of personal growth, and you're reading this book to continue learning, congratulations and welcome. If you got this book because there's someone else in your life who "needs it," welcome too, and please read on; maybe you'll find something in here that you can use to help them. And, while you're at it, it never hurts to take a little of your own advice.

Have a great life!

Contents

Part I: Life

Part II: Liberty

Part III: The Pursuit of Happiness

PART I

◆

LIFE

1

◆

This Is Your Life

There is only one success—to be able to spend your life in your own way.

—Christopher Morley

I called this first section *Life*, although I'm not going to cover the entire subject here. In particular, I'm not going to address the question of how you *should* live your life. That's a question for philosophers, and to me a fairly impractical question: after all, how many people do you see living their lives just as they *should?* Instead, I'm going to talk about how you *do* live your life.

Early human beings used to spend an awful lot of time and energy just surviving. When we weren't busy with moment-to-moment survival—eating, raising children, running from predators, sleeping—we were busy securing survival for the future—building shelter, hunting, farming, or (later in history) making money to see us through hard times.

As ultimate testimony to how good a job we did, we now find ourselves with something called *leisure time*. It's pretty amazing: we got so good at taking care of our survival and security that nowadays we have time, energy, and perhaps money left over. Now this is very, very recent in the scheme of things, at least for people other than kings and that ilk, but the fact is, if you're reading this book, you've got leisure time. Congratulations.

The great thing about leisure time is you can do anything you want with it: read, go for a walk, wear leisure suits—whatever. If you don't have much leisure time at this point in your life, we'll work on that in the *Liberty* section, but for now, here's a pop quiz: how much of your leisure time do you spend having a truly satisfying, fulfilling experience of life? How much is it? If it's not 100%, why not? This is your free time, after all! If your answer was close to 100%—congratulations! And imagine what it would be like to have that kind of experience the rest of your day, too—in your job, in your relationships—it's possible!

How big a slice of your leisure time is genuinely fulfilling?

4

The only thing standing between you and a fantastically fulfilling life is a lack of the proper tools—tools to help you structure your life so you can fulfill your own unique set of needs. Our schools and universities simply don't teach that. They range from mediocre to excellent at turning out productive citizens—"productive" meaning good at survival and security, and at perpetuating the society that produced them. But there isn't much in the curriculum about having a high-quality life while you're doing it.

I had the privilege of going to college at Harvard University. Harvard has been fantastically successful, both at turning out famous graduates and at perpetuating itself. I went there because it had a reputation as the world's best college. Because so many people want to go there, based on its reputation, they admit only those applicants showing the most intelligence and talent. Because those people generally become successful, they become living advertisements for the school, drawing in the next generation of students and donating generously in response to the school's annual plea for contributions.

While we did manage to learn a bit from the lectures, most alumni I have talked with about our Harvard education agree the best thing about going to school there was meeting so many great people as our classmates. We could have had almost the same benefit without involving Harvard at all if we had just rented a clubhouse somewhere!

We human beings—and our educational institutions—have become experts at surviving. We spend billions of dollars each year and employ some of our most brilliant researchers in learning more and more about how to survive longer—how to eat healthier, how to prevent and cure more diseases, how to build a healthy body and repair it surgically when it fails—we are superb at that.

That's fine. So, now that we have that handled, how about addressing the question of what to do with all those healthy years of survival? There's more to it than just making it through—isn't there?

At the risk of giving away the surprise ending, I'll answer that question: Yes, there is more to life than surviving until death. I'm

5

not saying survival isn't important: get survival handled. Get regular checkups. Eat healthy. Floss. Do all that stuff. But when it comes to the part of your life you don't need to devote purely to survival, you have a choice: What do you want your life to be about? Maybe you've thought about this and maybe you haven't. But I think it's fair to say:

> Everybody wants a great life—a totally fulfilling, satisfying life by their own standards—but most people, even if they believe it's possible, don't know how to get it.

It *is* possible, and we're going to find out how.

SELF-RELIANCE

Just before I left home for Harvard at the age of 17, my father decided to share with me some of his wisdom to see me on my way. He died a few years later, and I remember him as a warm, energetic man who devoted his life to healing children emotionally and mentally, and who made up nicknames for everyone he liked.

He had shared his wisdom with me before on several occasions, usually while listening to a Red Sox game and drinking a few Gablinger's Special Draft 66-calorie beers (drinking light beers before they became mainstream, he was truly a man ahead of his time). This wisdom usually consisted of a neat little rule-of-life he had determined to be significant: "Son," he would tell me, nodding his head slightly and lifting his bushy gray eyebrows as if to distance them from his much more pronounced, but similarly textured, mustache, "never bet on a filly who fades in the stretch."

I'm not sure if he was giving me advice about his favorite

hobby, horse racing, or if it was a subtle message relating to any marriage plans in my future. In any case, on this one occasion, I remember asking him how he had decided to become a child psychologist. My father, more serious than usual, though not stern, and still with the light beer in his hand that served as a prerequisite for the imparting of wisdom, told me he hoped I would read Ralph Waldo Emerson's essay "Self-Reliance" while I was at college. He told me reading it had been a turning point in his life, had helped him decide what to do with his life and, more importantly, how to live it.

Although through some combination of rebellion and procrastination I didn't actually read Emerson's essay for more than ten years from that talk, I did come to a similar turning point in my life as the result of taking my first personal-growth workshop. (Having done both, I can safely say that taking a workshop is a far more effective means of learning than reading an essay, especially one written in 19th-Century English.)

Emerson wrote about people's fear of trusting themselves. He saw that so much failure and misery in the world was a result of people failing to trust their own judgment. Yet the ironic thing is:

> We are always making our own decisions.

Either that or we make our own *indecisions,* which often lead to worse consequences than active decisions. In a way, not making a decision is a decision too.

If we let others decide for us—then we've *decided* to let others decide for us, and that's also our own decision. And while it's fine to delegate decisions to others when they have more information or experience than we do, often we simply do it out of habit or out of fear that our own decision wouldn't be good enough.

Have you ever had a thought or idea but kept it to yourself or not acted on it because you didn't trust the worthiness of your own idea? Have you ever then heard the same idea come out of someone else's mouth and suddenly felt a wave of emotion—justification, gratification, or even humiliation or resentment because you knew it was your idea first? Your ideas are just as good as anyone's! I've heard it said everybody has at least two million-dollar ideas in a lifetime. What do you think separates the people who make the million dollars from the rest of us?

Action! Those people rely on themselves, trust themselves, and act! The rest of us have plenty of excuses, reasons why we don't trust ourselves, justifications for not acting—but in the end, we don't even get the *chance* to make those great ideas into reality.

> Self-reliance means trusting ourselves to know what's important, casting aside excuses, and going for it!

ADVICE AND ROLE MODELS

Self-reliance does not, of course, mean you have to sit in a room by yourself and never listen to anyone else's opinion. Although I consider myself self-reliant, much of my success comes from my willingness to learn from others. But there are some perils involved in taking advice, primarily when it comes to the question of whose advice is worth taking.

Fortunately, I do have some advice for you on the subject of taking advice, which is:

> Only take advice from people with lives you like.

If someone gives you advice, and the advice is sincere, you have to assume following the advice will help make your life *more like theirs*. So:

- Take advice on relationships from people with good relationships.
- Take advice on investing your money from people who have successfully invested their own money.
- Take advice on how to work effectively from people who work effectively.

Sometimes much more advice is forthcoming from people who *don't* fit this criterion than people who do. Be selective! Before I got married, I got lots of advice from single people that I should wait, back off, be more careful. My married friends just smiled. I remember telling one friend, a highly intelligent, sensitive, caring, but *divorced* woman of 50, that with all due respect, I would take my advice on how to have relationships that work from people who had relationships that worked! Fortunately, being enlightened, she saw the humor in it.

So don't just take my advice—even if you imagine I lead an attractive life. Think about it. Make it make sense to you, and if it does, make the advice come from you, not me. I sincerely believe that the ideas in this book can make the difference between a life of bouncing between The Pits and OK, and a life of pushing the needle way past OK into uncharted delight and fulfillment. If it makes sense to you, do it.

Before I made the decision to trust my own judgment about how to live my life, I searched long and hard for an answer, for someone else to tell me how I *should* live it. I was hungry for advice, and the more I got, the more confused I became. I tried to be like my role models, to copy the way they acted and talked because it was clear to me they were powerful, fulfilled people. I copied their actions, but the real secret of their success never occurred to me: in those qualities that I admired and in those areas where they succeeded, *they trusted their own judgment.*

I saw they were confident, so I acted confident—but that didn't get me the fulfillment I saw in them. They really *were* confident, because they trusted themselves. I saw they were sure of what they wanted, so I set my sights on the same kinds of things they wanted—but that didn't get me fulfillment. They really *wanted* those things, and they knew they wanted them, because they trusted themselves.

No matter how perfectly I copied the people I admired and envied, and even if I succeeded in getting the results that they got, it didn't get me the experience of life I wanted. Why? Because I was a different person and I wanted different things. Did I know what I wanted? Not really. But since I didn't rely on myself to know what was best for me, I didn't even bother to figure it out.

If you don't trust yourself to know what's best for you, because you're afraid you might be wrong, then whom or what do you trust? It's good to know—they'll be running your life until you change your mind. They'll have all your power, and they'll be the ones to decide whether you do something worthwhile with your life, or whether you simply pace off the minutes from here to the end of the line. And if you don't feel you are trustworthy—if you're living your life based on some kind of weighted average of all the advice you've been given from kindergarten until now—well, whose decision was it to do that?

It was yours. At least, it's yours now. If you've never thought about this before and therefore never had a chance to make the decision to trust yourself—why not make that decision right now?

You are always trusting yourself, anyway, on some level; the final decision, or lack of one, always comes down to you. Why not cut through the confusion, the distortion, the doubt, resentment, and fear? Why not trust directly in your own inner sense of what is right and wrong, good and bad, worthwhile and worthless? This is *your* life. Why not rely on yourself?

2

◆

Choices

Believe it or not.

—*Robert Leroy Ripley*

If you've made the choice to rely on yourself to know what's best for you—and I hope you have, because otherwise there's not much point in reading the rest of this book—it's time to take a look at the different kinds of choices you have in your life. No matter what situation you are in, *you always have a choice.* It may not always be a choice between great prizes on a game show, but you always have a choice.

If this seems unrealistic, let's take an example. Think of something in your everyday life that you don't want to do but you *have to*—that you have no choice about. Pick something that personally feels like an obligation such as "I have to take out the garbage," not a law of nature such as "night has to follow day." When you've thought of something, read on.

OK, so now you've thought of something you feel like you have to do; maybe you said "I have to go to work." Now ask yourself, why? What would happen if you didn't? Chances are you'll come up with one or more highly undesirable things that would happen if you didn't do that thing that you "have to" do. For instance, if I didn't go to work:

- I wouldn't get paid.
- My house would be repossessed.
- My family would be thrown out on the street.
- My mother would yell at me.
- etc.

Work this through with your own example. What would happen if you didn't do the thing you "have to" do?

While these things may be so unthinkable or unpleasant that you would never consciously choose them over the "have-to" thing, you *do* actually have a choice. If someone's holding a gun to my head and demanding my wallet, I have a choice: my money or my life! Easy choice, I hope, although neither alternative seems too appealing at the time. So even with the things you "have to" do, you are really *choosing* to do them.

My point is, if all your possible choices seem crummy, then if you pick the least crummy choice, you've done yourself a favor. Pat yourself on the back—you've done something far more effective than sitting around resenting the fact that you don't like any of your choices. You've made the best choice available; you might as well feel good about it.

Choices are power. The more choices you realize you have, the more power you have, so it's important to know that you do *always* have choice. If you want, take some time and work through some more examples of things you feel like you have to do, and discover what the alternatives are and that you are really choosing to do them. Some examples you might try are:

- I have to obey the law.
  (If I don't obey the law, I risk going to jail or being fined, losing my reputation, and having my friends reject me. Therefore I am choosing to obey the law.)
- I have to treat my parents with honor and respect.
  (If I don't . . .)
- I have to do the dishes.
- I have to keep my opinion of my boss to myself.
- I have to spend time with my family.
- I have to fill my car up with gas.

> You always have a choice.

CONSCIOUS AND UNCONSCIOUS CHOICES

You always have a choice, but it's not always so easy to take advantage of that knowledge. One problem is that not all the choices we make are explicit or conscious. Sometimes the choice goes right by before we even realize we made one.

Your brain is a big choice-making machine. Some of your choices are conscious, and you're well aware you're making them: what to have for lunch, which movie to see, what time to set your alarm clock for. But most choices you make unconsciously: If you're walking, you don't consciously think, "OK, I'll move my right foot.

Now the left. Now right again . . ." Your brain is constantly making unconscious choices about such things as how to walk, when to breathe, how to move your lips when you talk, when to get angry. When you make a choice based on intuition, or "gut feeling," that's a combination—you are consciously choosing to let your unconscious make the choice for you: often a wise idea, considering your unconscious has access to a lot more material than your conscious ever has at any one time!

Why do two people make different choices in the same situation? Often it is because they have a different set of *unconscious* attitudes, opinions, beliefs, and values. The choices you make every moment of every day, even the conscious ones, are greatly influenced by this set of unconscious items. Since choices are power, it's well worth investing some time in exploring your unconscious and discovering more about what's in there.

When I talk about your unconscious, all I mean is the part of you that is not actively thinking—the passive part, the part that has your home phone number stored in it, ready for you to bring it to consciousness when you need it. The conscious part of you is the part you are always aware of. If you're thinking to yourself, "OK, get to the point, I learned this in Sixth Grade," that's a conscious thought. But before you started reading this section, that knowledge was unconscious (it's probably been there since Sixth Grade).

When we learn something, we often start our learning consciously; then, as we become adept, we allow the learning to back off into our unconscious. For example, when I learned to read Spanish, I started off by translating each word consciously to its English counterpart, then putting the English words together to get the meaning of the sentence. Later, as I became more skilled, I could just read many sentences and understand the meaning without consciously translating each word.

So when I'm talking about the unconscious part of you, I mean everything you ever learned, all the memories of everything you ever did or thought, all your beliefs about the way the world works, all your attitudes and opinions about every subject—wow! There's a lot of stuff in there! Important stuff, because what's in your unconscious is the main thing that differentiates your mind from a baby's. A baby has to spend all its conscious energy doing the simplest things—moving its arms and legs, crawling, walking—toilet training! Your grown-up unconscious lets you do all that without even thinking.

Here's my point: Your unconscious is an enormous collection of learnings, beliefs, attitudes, experiences, strategies, patterns, and miscellany, and it has an appropriately enormous influence on your life, on how you perceive things, and on the millions of little choices you make every day.

That's why most attempts to change behavior—for example, lose weight—by "will power" (conscious thought) don't work in the long term. Suppose you manage to stay conscious of your intention to exercise, eat less, etc., and follow through with the unpleasant chores (unpleasant because you are fighting your unconscious) long enough to establish a new unconscious pattern of behavior. As soon as you drop your will power and focus your energy on something else (there is probably something else worth focusing on in life besides dieting), the new unconscious pattern will have to fight against whatever parts of your unconscious didn't want you to diet in the first place, and will probably lose the battle.

You can go a long way by understanding how your unconscious works well enough to get it to support you, rather than fight against you, in your priorities in life. Make sure you're making good unconscious choices as well as good conscious choices.

MAKING THE MOST OF YOUR UNCONSCIOUS

Consider the entire set of everything you believe, both consciously and unconsciously. This includes everything from your name to the multiplication table to your political beliefs. These beliefs get into our brains in a variety of ways:

- We learn them from our parents.
- We learn them in school or through religious training.
- We read them in a book, newspaper, or magazine.
- We get them from television or movies.
- We hear something repeatedly and unconsciously learn it.
- We make observations and draw conclusions.
- We are punished or told we will be punished for not believing.
- We adopt beliefs from people we respect or fear.

We are incredible learners! Even if you don't consider yourself a good learner, if you can read this, you are. Just think what you needed to learn to get from birth, not knowing the English language or the shapes of letters, to where you are now, having learned to look at black marks on white paper and translate them into ideas!

You learned every belief, attitude, and opinion you now hold between the time you were born (or maybe conceived—some parents practice in-the-womb education these days) and right now. You learned most of them without even realizing it, by absorbing the beliefs and attitudes around you throughout your life. As life went on, you changed or even reversed some beliefs or attitudes, either consciously or unconsciously.

Are you a person with many strongly held beliefs, clear about them and happy with the way your life works under them? Or are you someone with nothing you would call an unshakable belief—you consider yourself open-minded about absolutely everything? (Or would that be an unshakable belief in itself?) You could be somewhere in between, or even be in a total state of confusion. I'm not recommending one extreme over the other here, although I will stick my neck out and recommend clarity over confusion.

The key is to understand one thing:

> You can choose your beliefs.

You can choose your opinions and attitudes too. If we were *conscious* of all our attitudes, opinions, and beliefs it would be easy to see which ones were in conflict with our most important priorities so we could do something about them. The trick is to find those *unconscious* ones that are stuck in there but not doing us any good. Those undesirable beliefs get into our unconscious in many ways:

- Leftovers from the past.
- Watching television commercials.
- Watching television programs.
- Hearing bad news. (It travels fast!)
- Rubbing off from people you live or work with who are making poor choices in their own lives.
- Myths.
- Old sayings.
- Intentional manipulation by people or institutions that want something from you.
- Beliefs put out, intentionally or unintentionally, by people whose lives you do not find particularly appealing.

Wouldn't it be nice to get a list of all the unconscious beliefs and attitudes you have, along with an explanation of where you got them, so you could go through it with a thick marker and line-item veto the ones you don't want? Unfortunately, the brain doesn't work that way. But when you do become conscious of an attitude or belief that keeps getting in your way, you have the choice to change it.

> You can choose to change any attitude, opinion, or belief that conflicts with something you're clear is more important.

YOUR CONTEXT

The complete set of any one person's attitudes, opinions, beliefs, and myths is her *context.* For instance, when you saw I used the word "her" in the last sentence for a person of unknown sex, what did you think or feel? You may have felt uncomfortable or hostile, perhaps due to a belief that the choice of "his" would have been grammatically correct. Maybe you were pleased or felt closer to me because you believe people who use bias-free language are friends, or trustworthy. Or did you feel manipulated, perhaps holding an attitude that men who bend over backward to use "politically correct" language are being manipulative? Could be you didn't even notice it.

None of these responses is "correct," of course. But the point is different people reading exactly the same sentence respond

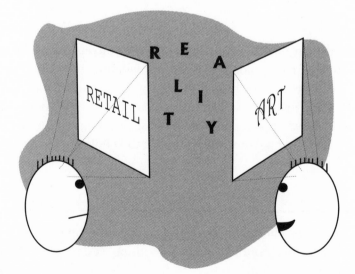

Different people looking at the same reality through different contexts perceive different things, leading to different feelings, choices, and results.

differently, and their response is determined by their context: the complete set of attitudes and beliefs they have at the moment they read the sentence.

Your context changes constantly, whether you are trying to change it deliberately or not. If you don't believe me, go back and re-read that sentence and notice what reaction you have to the word "her" this time. Try it now!

If you had a different reaction this time, it's because you changed your context. You have some new beliefs, even in this short time; in particular, you probably believe I stuck that word in there deliberately to make a point. If you were offended before, maybe you're amused now. If you felt warm or trusting before, maybe you feel put off or a little betrayed knowing I had a hidden agenda.

I don't want to make too big a deal out of this little example, and of course few people are particularly concerned with how they react to the word "her," whether I put it in there intentionally or not. But just look at the difference in how people feel about and judge this little tiny thing! Imagine what a difference your context makes in how you view your job, or a personal relationship. Is there a difference in how you feel and respond if you believe someone offended you on purpose rather than by accident? Does it feel different to do a chore if you believe you are appreciated rather than being taken advantage of? That's why it's so important to know more about your context and how it affects your life.

CHOICES ABOUT THE PAST

While choices about the future are limited only by our imagination and resources, we have far less choice about the past. As difficult as it sometimes is to change a present situation we have gotten into, changing the past is *impossible*. The only real choice we have about the past is to change our present point of view about what happened: to change our context about the past.

If you find yourself stuck regretting, resenting, or dwelling on the past—is that the best choice of how to be spending your energy right now? How about taking the point of view that you made the best choices you knew how to make at the time, and turning your attention to the present?

If you look back in hindsight and say, "No way—that wasn't the best choice I could have made," be careful! That *was* the choice you made, consciously or unconsciously. Unless you learn something new, you're likely to make the same choice again in a similar situation. That's where personal growth, greater awareness, and increased understanding of yourself come in.

I am not saying to put on blinders and be a Pollyanna, ignoring reality. ("Oh, what a beautiful day! I got a ticket coming to work, the boss yelled at me, I slipped and fell in the garbage, and everything's just fine!") I am trying to get you excited about the possibility that by understanding how your context works, you can make it work to your advantage.

> We make the best choices we can, given who we are and what we know. To make better choices—know more!

3

◆

Nature, Nurture, and Culture

A young Daughter asked her Mother why she always cut the ends off the roast before putting it into the oven. "Well, that's the way Grandma taught me," Mother replied. But Mother herself was unsure of the reason, so she passed the question on to the girl's Grandma. "That's just the way my mother used to make them," Grandma replied. But now Grandma too was curious, and next time she saw Great-Grandma, who was very old but still in good health and great spirits, she asked her, "Mother, why did you always cut the ends off the roast before you put it in the oven?" Great-Grandma's eyes sprung open. She laughed lightly, shook her head, and answered, "That danged oven was so small you couldn't fit a thing in there. Cutting the ends off the roast was the only way to make it fit."

—Old Wives' Tale

We often hear we are the product of our genes and our environment: "nature" and "nurture." While the same can be said of all organisms—trees and snakes, tigers and snails—we humans have an interesting feature that separates us from the other life forms: our conscious minds.°

When I talk about what distinguishes us, I'm not just saying we can learn new things—you don't need consciousness for that. Rats learn to run mazes. Dogs learn new tricks. Ant colonies "learn" where food is when individual ants leave a chemical trail. It's not just that we can learn, or even that we are the best learners of all the organisms. Our consciousness gives us a greater gift even than that: the gift of conscious choice.

> One of our greatest gifts as human beings is the gift of conscious choice.

We don't necessarily *use* the gift of conscious choice as much as we might. I've gone on unconscious auto-pilot more than once and, for example, driven my car halfway to work before I realized my wife and I were headed out to dinner. Sometimes we leave our gift of consciousness gift-wrapped in the closet.

We have the unique(?) ability to make conscious choices.

° Some people believe non-humans such as chimpanzees, cats, dolphins, or trees may also be conscious. If that's true, and they want to borrow your copy of this book so they can have fantastic lives too, go ahead and let them.

Even so, consciousness greatly aided our survival early in history. The first people with consciousness genes survived and reproduced better, making those genes spread rapidly at the expense of people/humanoids without them. Consciousness gave us the ability to imagine ourselves fending off saber-tooth tigers with a club, thus strengthening our position in the prehistoric power structure. (That this occurred can be historically verified by watching The Flintstones.) Our technological advantage continued to increase to the point where we quickly eliminated any threat to our survival from creatures big enough to swing a club at, and nowadays we have eliminated most threats, including diseases, that would keep us from replicating our genes. Yay!

THE BEGINNINGS OF CULTURE

An interesting thing happened, though, as our newly evolved consciousness propelled our rise to earthly power. Suddenly, for the first time in prehistory, there was a new way to replicate information besides genetically. This was very exciting for human people, although they didn't know it yet. The term usually used to describe this whole set of non-genetic information is "culture."

So why is it a big deal that a new way to replicate information showed up? First off, if you believe in evolution, it's certainly an interesting event.° Things started changing a lot faster than they had before, at least in the recent past.

For millions of years, genetic evolution had cranked on slowly, with variations and rare mutations modifying the DNA information over the patient course of many generations. A space alien who dropped in on the planet a million years ago, then stopped by again a century later, wouldn't have seen too much change in what our

---

° If you don't believe in evolution, I recommend you read Richard Dawkins's books *The Selfish Gene* and *The Blind Watchmaker,* which give a thoroughly convincing explanation of genetic evolution. You may change your mind!

planet's inhabitants did on a Saturday night, or in anything else for that matter.

The evolution of information carried by *consciousness* is much, much faster: while genes evolve over the course of many genera-tions—hundreds or thousands of years—*ideas* evolve over the course of years, days, or even minutes. Today, the effect on the planet of human cultural evolution *so outweighs* the changes made by genetic evolution as to make genetic evolution insignificant. (One might argue that it's insignificant to us as individual people anyway, since none of it will happen during a single lifetime.)

What kind of information is this, replicated so much faster than DNA? Am I talking about books, photocopied in a library and passed around? Am I talking about television programs, broadcast to millions of sets simultaneously and then transmitted to millions of brains? Am I talking about the kind of bad news that travels fast—a politician's rumored extramarital affair or the start of a war?

I am talking about any information that is good at replicating itself. Obviously, the information itself has no consciousness, no conscious intent to replicate itself any more than the DNA does. What I'm simply saying is that some information—some knowledge, beliefs, attitudes, myths, facts, positions, plans, designs, even songs or lines from movies—just happens to get passed around, while other information doesn't. Any piece of information that gets replicated—genetically or otherwise—is called a *meme* (rhymes with dream).

MEMES AND CULTURE

Some elements of the United States culture containing successful memes—from a meme's point of view, "successful" means it survives and spreads—are: the English language, the Bible, movie stars' names, driving a car, shaking hands, wearing clothes, money, The Beatles' songs, and credit cards. Some cultural elements with unsuccessful memes: names of non-celebrities, doodles drawn on those paper tablecloths at the finer restaurants with the provided crayons, thoughts kept to oneself and never acted upon, and cannibalism.

Just as some genes led to increased chances for survival and reproduction in their host organisms, so do some memes lead to the survival and/or spreading of the culture or subculture that contains them. If you examine any culture, religion, or institution that has endured for many years or has spread significantly, you will always find one or more memes at work causing the survival or the spread. Here are some common memes that are components of cultures, religions, or institutions that have endured or grown:

Evangelism: The belief that it is of prime importance to persuade others to adopt a belief system. This causes a constant outpouring of energy directed at "spreading the word" and thus propagating the meme. Evangelism is a very, very successful meme in terms of replicating itself and the cultures of which it is part. It is found in such varied institutions as Fundamentalist Christianity and Apple Computer Co., the latter actually having an executive with the title "software evangelist," whose mission is to persuade software companies of the importance of developing computer programs for Apple's computers.

Elitism: The belief that a certain culture, way of life, group of people, etc., is the *best, chosen,* or *elect.* For individuals who are current believers, this meme can justify suffering and create a reluctance to leave the institution. It's also attractive to prospective members. Found in many religions, including Judaism, and also at two highly elite institutions I have personal experience with: Harvard University and Microsoft Corporation.

Fear of Punishment: The belief that non-believers or those who jump ship will be punished. This punishment can take place either quickly and verifiably, as in the case of losing wages or stock options by quitting a company, or in the afterlife, where it is more difficult to disprove and usually as unpleasant as possible. The punishment is often simply the disapproval of the other believers. The worse the threatened punishment, the greater the fear, and the more suffering the believer is willing to endure rather than risk punishment.

Crisis: The belief that we are currently in a crisis and that it is of prime importance to act now and to tell as many people as possible before it's too late. This meme was once a valuable weapon against saber-tooth tigers, and today keeps many news organizations, talk shows, and politicians in business. In the 1992 presidential election, challenger Bill Clinton beat incumbent George Bush on the strength of Clinton's message that the United States was, in fact, having several crises including health care and the budget deficit, and that we'd better change presidents before it was too late. Putting aside the question of who was right, Bush's counter-message—that in fact the economy was already rebounding and that health care wasn't that bad—wasn't nearly as successful at spreading, because it didn't have good memes in it.

*News relating to a crisis spreads faster than other
kinds of news because of the successful "crisis" meme.*

Tradition: The belief that it is important to do and believe the same thing that has been done and believed before. Non-evangelical religions such as Judaism have a strong Tradition meme. The US justice system, based on precedent and case law rather than individual judges' gut feelings of what would be just in each case, requires skyscraperfuls of lawyers to support and interpret all its traditions.

Low risk, high reward: The belief that the possibility of a great reward, even if it is unlikely, outweighs the low risk or cost of a belief or action. People play the state lottery and throw pennies in wishing wells because of this meme. William James said it was illogical not to believe in God, because the possible reward of believing in Him was enormous and the cost was nil. (Of course, that assumes you haven't been exposed to a religion that preaches eternal damnation for believers and paradise only for atheists!)

SUCCESSFUL MEMES AREN'T NECESSARILY TRUE

These are just some of the core beliefs that are part of many popular cultural institutions. I find this topic fascinating, but let me bring it back to the point of this book, which is having a great life. If you want a great life, it helps to realize the question of whether a belief is widespread, long-standing, or successful at replicating itself is a completely separate question from whether the belief is *true.*

> Information, beliefs, attitudes, or myths may be prevalent, or may have been around for a long time, but that doesn't make them true.

Of course, they *might* be true, but not necessarily, and it's good to know the difference. In fact, since memes evolve so much faster than genes, we can't even assume that just because a belief system is prevalent or has been around for hundreds or thousands of years, that it is *good for us as individuals or as human beings!* All we know is that it's good at replicating itself!

Chain letters are a great illustration of how things can spread if they contain good memes, regardless of their truth or benefit. There's one chain letter I have personally received twice, and which I have seen written up in newspaper articles, that will not seem to die—and no wonder: it has practically every kind of successful meme in it! It begins something like this:

> Congratulations on your good fortune! This letter brings
> incredible good luck to everyone who receives it and
> passes it on to 20 friends *[evangelism]* within 48 hours of
> receiving it *[crisis]*. It has been around the world nine
> times *[tradition]*. Many people do not believe in the
> power of this good-luck letter, but those who do believe
> are rewarded *[elitism]*.
>
> Myrtle Gottsmertz of Fort Wayne, New Jersey, inherited
> one million dollars three days after receiving this letter
> and passing it on *[low risk, high reward]*. Fred Wympfish
> of Dallas, Texas found $12,000 in cash two hours after
> receiving this letter, but didn't pass it on and was killed by
> a falling piano three days later *[fear of punishment]*.

Wow! With a beginning like that, the rest of it could probably have said anything at all and it would still work. Notice that someone had to start the thing, and obviously made it up out of whole cloth when they did, since none of it could have happened yet. Maybe someone was doing a research project on memes?

My whole point here is: give yourself permission to examine your beliefs. I'm not saying throw them away; not at all! I just want you to notice that beliefs spread in ways that are not particularly related either to how true they are or to how useful having the belief is to you, your family, your society, or the world.

Don't be a slave to a meme! These self-replicating ideas often do not have your best interests at heart. Choose your own context and run your own life!

4

◆

Models and Truth

A boy walking down a city street sees an old man standing in a doorway, looking from side to side and snapping his fingers. After watching the old man for several minutes, the boy goes up to him and asks, "Hey, old man, how come you keep snapping your fingers?" The old man, still swinging his head from side to side, says, "Keeps the tigers away." The boy pipes up, "There aren't any tigers in the city!" The old man, still snapping, looks at him knowingly. "See, it works!"

—*Vaudeville Shtick*

If what I say today contradicts what I said yesterday, it is not because I do not speak the truth; but, rather, as I grow and change, my truth changes from day to day.

—*Mohandas K. Gandhi (paraphrased)*

Have you ever wondered why Einstein's Theory of Relativity is called a "theory" rather than a fact? Are scientists in doubt about it? Are they waiting until they've proved it beyond a shadow of a doubt before they remove the "theory" label and promote it to the ranks of accepted knowledge? Actually, no. As I write this, scientists are fairly happy at least with what Einstein called his "Special" theory of relativity—a theory about the way things behave when they move around relative to each other—a theory which, incidentally, contradicts the theory of Sir Isaac Newton, a smart fellow who invented much of Calculus in his spare time.

The reason these scientific ideas are called theories, not facts, is because in science, the only facts are the observed results of experiments. Anything that does a good job of explaining those results and predicting the results of new experiments is called a theory or model. Observations are facts; explanations are theories.

Even though Newton's theory predicted most experimental results correctly for 300 years, Einstein did not accept it as Truth and stop thinking; he looked for and found a better theory that was even more accurate and useful to physicists. As far as we know, Einstein's theory is true, although it has yet to be fully integrated with quantum mechanics. Newton's is close, but not quite.

The problem is, while Einstein's theory predicts more accurately than Newton's how objects behave when they are moving extremely fast, using it involves multiplying a lot of big numbers and taking square roots. It's just not worth it when you're dealing with situations in your everyday life, such as how fast your car is going relative to the speed limit. Since your car is not going close to the speed of light, even if you live in California, figuring your speed using Newton's view of the world would be so accurate that no known measuring device could tell the difference from Einstein's "true" calculation.

WAYS TO LOOK AT LIFE

This book is about ways to look at life. Everything I talk about here is a model, not a Truth: the trick is to find the models of life that help the most with your personal priorities. Most any model of life will agree with the big, indisputable truths of reality. The difference comes from the attitudes, opinions and beliefs you have when the truth is not absolutely clear. Here are some examples of what I'm talking about—different, sometimes contradictory attitudes, where choosing the one in alignment with your goals might make a big difference:

A rolling stone gathers no moss.	Still water runs deep.
He who hesitates is lost. A stitch in time saves nine. You snooze, you lose! Strike while the iron is hot.	Haste makes waste. Look before you leap. Fools rush in where angels fear to tread.
The squeaky wheel gets the grease. Ask and you shall receive.	Better to keep your mouth shut and let people think you are a fool than to open it and let them know.
Birds of a feather flock together.	Opposites attract.
Never judge a book by its cover.	Beauty is in the eye of the beholder
When in Rome, do as the Romans do.	March to the beat of a different drummer.
All that glitters is not gold.	Where there's smoke, there's fire.
The race goes to the swift.	Slow 'n' steady wins the race.
Keep your nose to the grindstone, your shoulder to the wheel.	All work and no play makes Jack a dull boy.
No pain, no gain.	Go with the flow.
Gather ye rosebuds while ye may.	Stop and smell the roses.
If at first you don't succeed, try, try again.	Fool me once, shame on you; fool me twice, shame on me!
Absence makes the heart grow fonder. Familiarity breeds contempt.	Out of sight, out of mind. While the cat's away, the mice will play.
You can't teach an old dog new tricks.	You're never too old to change.

Why are there so many old sayings that contradict each other, and which ones are "true"? The answer is that it's not a question of true or false. Using any of these as a rule of thumb in an appropriate situation could work well to help you with your priorities. Using any one of them as an excuse or justification to avoid something you want to do, but are afraid to, will not work well for you.

> It's not a matter of figuring out what life's rules are—different things work at different times! What's important is getting clear about what's most important to you and acting in accordance with it.

If adopting some opinion, attitude, or belief gets in your way—don't adopt it! If some attitude or belief you have is constantly getting in the way of what's most important to you, you might seriously want to reexamine it. Where did it come from, anyway?

LIFE'S LITTLE TRAINING WHEELS

My first bicycle came with training wheels. While I learned to ride, the training wheels kept me safe by preventing me from falling. The training wheels were definitely helping me at that stage. But as I learned to ride, and I started going faster and tearing around corners, I had to remove the training wheels, because what had once kept me safe was now getting in my way. It was scary, but I removed them and bike riding suddenly got a lot smoother and easier.

If some of our beliefs were as visible as training wheels, we would see a lot quicker when the time came to let go of them. As I grew up, an overweight loner among the neighborhood kids, I learned people were not to be trusted. When boys would approach me, it was often to insult me or beat me up. I learned quickly to harden myself, to avoid eye contact, to ignore taunts.

Although the severe hostility of that environment lasted only through junior high school, and in fact I met many people since then who wanted to be close to me, I rode around through life with the "training wheels" of my distrust for a long time after that. My point is this:

> Just because you have a belief, and nothing has happened to blatantly disprove it, *that doesn't mean the belief is true!*

People and life are so varied and complicated that it's rare that one universal statement of "Truth" is always true for everyone and for all of time. In fact, a belief may be working against you in the form of self-fulfilling prophecy. Beliefs such as "I can't _____" or "I'm too _____ to do _____" are obvious examples: just by believing those things, you affect the results you get in all sorts of ways. But there are many more subtle, unconscious beliefs we have that work against us until we recognize them and consciously develop new, more effective attitudes.

Beliefs or attitudes learned in the past can be like training wheels never removed from a bicycle, hindering us in improving our quality of life.

Early in school, we get taught facts and skills much as dogs get taught tricks. The model of education is: learn facts—truth—then prove you know them through a test, paper, presentation, or other means. After 12 or more years of this pattern, it's not surprising it's tough to shake, especially considering we do learn a lot of valuable things in school. Without mastering the basic fundamentals of language, arithmetic, and problem-solving, it's difficult to get along today.

But that doesn't mean I'm going to go unconscious and run on auto-pilot, spending the rest of my days learning facts and proving to other people I know them. Do you know people like that? I've met folks who, for no purpose apparent to me, spend their lives doing just that—learning facts and proving they know them. If you're having trouble relating to this, go to a baseball park and listen to the conversations about batting averages, RBI's, and slugging percentages!

When I was an undergraduate at Harvard, there was a man who spent his life standing by the bus terminal in Harvard Square, listening to strangers' conversations and chiming in with the number of the bus they'd have to take to get to their destination. I tested his knowledge one day by asking him how to get to a particularly obscure location several miles away. Without missing a beat, he began, "ya gotta take *two* buses—"!

Most of us don't take the learning-telling pattern to quite this extreme. We make the transition from learning facts as an end in itself to abstract thinking—learning concepts, developing ways to think about life, building a belief system that helps us make sense of the world. New facts get filtered through this belief system and—in the traditional model of education—strengthen the true beliefs and bring into question the erroneous beliefs. By early adulthood, most of us have pretty much assembled the major beams and girders in our models of the universe, and continued acquisition of facts begins to have diminishing returns.

This is where most people stop unless they come upon some major crisis in their lives that requires rethinking some of their basic beliefs. It's not surprising: tinkering with your belief system can feel uncomfortable. So unless there's some good reason to do it, people tend to stick with what they've got. But "stick" is an appropriate word:

> Personal growth occurs when we allow our belief systems to flex and grow with us. When we develop an inflexible mindset, we stay stuck with what we've got.

What we've got may not be all that bad, but this book is not called "Getting to Not All That Bad." There are plenty of books you can read that will help you get to Not All That Bad. This book is about having an unimaginably *fantastic* life—we want to find out how to get *past* OK! That's going to require a new way of learning—but what other way to learn is there? It's kind of weird, isn't it? I mean—what is there besides Truth?

The way to make progress is to do what Einstein did. Just as he was willing to question something as obvious, unshakable, and "True" as Newton's Laws of Motion, the way to make real progress in life is to question attitudes and beliefs we consider "obviously true"—to realize there may be other, equally valid models of our life that, in our current situation, work better than the old one. Sometimes we need to do more unlearning than learning!

THE TRUTH TRAP

Have you ever read or heard about a foreign or ancient culture and laughed about some of the things they believed? Like that the Earth was carried on the back of a great turtle, or it was flat, or that the constellations of stars were formed by great battles among supernatural beings? Did you ever wonder how an entire culture could believe something that we now know so obviously to be untrue?

Well, guess what?

While most people agree there are some things that are absolutely, indisputably true—for example, that the Sun sets in the west, or that if I am hit by a fast-moving truck I am likely to be hurt—the vast, vast majority of beliefs people have are not the Indisputable, Universal Truth, but simply very strongly held opinions.

The trap comes when we mistake something that is true some of the time, or something that used to be true at one time in our lives, for the Absolute Universal Truth. As soon as we do that, all of a sudden we see everything else in the light of that Truth, and we start building a belief system. The belief system collects evidence to support itself, and becomes a filter through which we see things, and through which we make decisions in our lives.

My strategy used to be to go through life accumulating Truth. I figured by the time I was in college, I knew most of the Truth, and I would just fill in the gaps as I went along. I figured the more Truth I knew, the better life I would have. The trouble was, my life was getting more and more difficult. While I knew I was right, and could hold my own in an argument, I increasingly ran into people who weren't interested in arguing with me—or even being around me, for that matter—and my life didn't hold much satisfaction for me much of the time.

I had landed in the Truth Trap.

TRUTH AND GOLF

Imagine that my friends and I grow up playing golf using only a putter, and none of the other clubs. Every hole we tee off with the putter, hit the ball a few times on the fairway with the putter, and then, because of our great mastery of the club, one-putt most holes. We have a great time! Of course, many of our drives end up in the woods, but we've seen those other people play with their funny-looking clubs, and they hit them into the woods too! And they have to lug those big bags of clubs around!

You know, people come up to us all the time and try to convert us, but—well—we've always been putters, thank you very much. We believe in putting. To tell you the truth, and I'm a little ashamed to admit it, we actually make fun of those other people behind their backs. Boy, did someone ever sell them a bill of goods, getting them to carry all that baggage over 18 holes, just to wind up at the same place! I feel a little sorry for them—do you think they've been brainwashed? But I guess we're all entitled to our own beliefs.

TRUTH AND TRUST

Tough Tony and his friends grew up with the belief that people were not to be trusted. There are lots of ways they might have come by this belief, most likely that they had some untrustworthy people around when they were children. In any case, they continue through life being very careful not to put too much trust in people so as not to be hurt or taken advantage of.

Tony and his friends hang out at Java Joe's and look at the newspaper headlines, nodding knowingly at the stories about foolish people who were victims of fraud because they trusted someone. "You can't trust anyone," they say to each other with each new bit of evidence that comes in. "Nope, you can't be too careful."

After a few years of sipping coffee and reinforcing that belief, Tony becomes aware of another belief that seems true, based on his experience. "You know, I just don't seem to be able to get a break," he says, then pretty soon, "You can't win." This seems to be a popular belief, because he soon meets lots of other people who share it. They all hang out at Java Joe's and commiserate, watching the rich people drive by in the cars they bought with money they made by taking advantage of people. "Rich people are all jerks," they come to believe, and make even more friends. Tough Tony meets a nice woman at Java Joe's and they date a few times, but she breaks it off because she doesn't think she can trust him. Tony doesn't blame her. People aren't to be trusted.

THE SNOWBALL EFFECT

Do you see how, in both examples, the presence of one strong belief snowballs into additional attitudes and beliefs consistent with it? Pretty soon, all those attitudes start mutually supporting each other, providing evidence for the validity of the others, forming a fairly consistent belief system (or *context*) that produces certain decisions, behaviors, and results.

In the second example, our hero Tony starts off with a strong belief that people are not to be trusted. It doesn't matter at this point where that belief came from—as a kid growing up in the public schools in Newton, Massachusetts I certainly had ample justification for a similar belief. Anyway, our hero, believing people were not to be trusted and were trying to take advantage of him, was particularly wary of people trying to help him and overly suspicious of "opportunities" presented to him.

Since he is suspicious of opportunities and wary of people, he does not make a lot of changes, for better or for worse, in his life. After a while, he begins to notice he doesn't seem to be getting any breaks. Small wonder! He now becomes aware there are indeed some people who get breaks. Our brains love consistency, and so he (consciously or not) puzzles over why some people get breaks while he does not. Since he has a strong belief that people are not to be trusted, questioning whether those people who are getting breaks are more trusting than he is does not occur to him. Instead, he looks for other justifications. Aha! The ones who got breaks must have done it by taking advantage of people! His subconscious does a few consistency checks, then sees, yes, that fits the data. The urge for consistency is satisfied.

Well, now Tony has a new belief—that rich people *especially* are not to be trusted. Nothing happens to contradict that belief for a while—in fact, the stories he reads in the paper about the recent government scandals provide evidence to support it. And now he starts to develop a resentment and dislike for rich people. With that kind of context, how likely is he to make the changes necessary,

whatever they might be, to move closer to becoming rich himself—
to become something he hates?

I'm not saying the belief that people are not to be trusted is
false. And I'm not saying that it's *good* to trust people and *bad* not to
trust them. What I'm saying is that it's a point of view, an attitude.
Our unconscious minds are full of those kind of attitudes, and we
make our decisions in life based on the sum total of all the attitudes
and beliefs hanging around in there. So:

> Make sure your context is working for you, not against
> you.

A context full of strong opinions and beliefs can form a consistent,
seemingly "true" view of life, but keeps out new, useful points of view.

STOP COLLECTING EVIDENCE

Practically any point of view can be justified. It is possible to collect evidence to support almost any belief: if you want to believe people can't be trusted, you can find plenty of supporting evidence in the local newspaper alone. If you want to believe people are basically good and kind, you can find an abundance of evidence to support *that* belief in the same newspaper. Of course, for Tony this all happened unconsciously—his context filtered out the evidence that didn't fit in with his beliefs and let in the evidence that did.

It would be nice if there were a way to be truly unbiased and collect evidence fairly, uninfluenced by your existing beliefs. I don't know of any such way. No matter how open-minded you are, you look at the world through the filter of your context. You need to! How could you drive a car without your unconscious automatically telling you that the red light is something important, while ignoring the far greater expanse of green grass? For Tony, any situation where he could possibly get taken advantage of was a red light; his unconscious was filtering out the green grass of opportunities because it was programmed to believe they weren't as important.

> Your context *unconsciously* affects the way you perceive everything in life. Even if you *consciously* respond to every situation the best way you know how, your unconscious context has already stepped in and filtered out information you may never be aware of.

The best way to keep your context flexible enough to work with you, not against you, is to stop *consciously* collecting evidence to justify your beliefs. It's good to know what your beliefs are, but rather than justifying them by collecting evidence, leave them open to question if the need arises. The more you justify a belief by collecting evidence to support it, and the more you justify decisions based on that belief, the more entrenched that belief becomes in your mind. Soon, with whatever strong beliefs you happened to start out with serving as a seed, you end up with a crystallized mindset. Things pretty much fit together; they sort of make sense. You see the world through a filter of haphazardly acquired beliefs, attitudes, and opinions. And for most people up until now, the story ends there.

This is the Truth Trap: "What I believe is true. I can justify all my beliefs. If something I believe is proved to be wrong, I will admit my mistake; I'm rational and open-minded. I can justify my behavior based on my beliefs. I strive for consistency in my beliefs; to do otherwise would be hypocritical. I have integrity, morality, and values all based on my beliefs and live life by them."

Huh? That's a trap? Wait a minute—that last paragraph describes some of the most successful, upstanding people we know! What could be wrong with that?

Nothing is "wrong" with it. That does indeed describe the mindset of some of the most admired and successful people on earth. Some of them, not all. And it's not a bad place to be! I am all in favor of integrity, morality, and values, not to mention rationality, open-mindedness, and truth. If you identified with the sentiment of that paragraph, you are in a very good place—you are poised for a major breakthrough in the quality of your life. Because there is another way to look at the same thing.

ESCAPE FROM THE TRUTH TRAP

Consider the following statement:

"There are any number of models of the universe—any number of points of view to look at each situation. I can choose the models and points of view that work for me in each situation to support what is most important to me, rather than stick with one model or point of view out of a desire for consistency. I am clear about what is most important to me, and choose my context to support me in that."

Notice the difference in the statements. In the first, the primary consideration is a reliance on the truth or accuracy of the way you currently look at life. There's nothing wrong with that, and yet the second point of view is even more powerful. Why? Because the primary consideration is for *what is most important to you,* not your current model of life.

In my experience, the people who are the most sure and trusting about their model of life are the ones who have the most to gain by shifting to the second way to look at things—by shifting their orientation from "How does what is happening make sense according to my understanding of life?" to "Which of the many possible ways to look at this situation supports me in what is most important to me?"

Sometimes we make clinging to our current model of life more important than our quality of life. The more willing you are to question—and possibly change—beliefs or attitudes that you have, the easier it is to live with integrity around what is truly most important to you.

> Integrity means believing, speaking, and acting in accordance with what is truly most important to you, even if it contradicts what you did, said, or believed in the past.

OUR HERO ESCAPES

Here's the epilogue to Tough Tony's story: After reading this book, our hero Tony realized his lack of trust was getting in the way of some important things he wanted in life, so he made a decision. He decided to change his point of view about trusting people. But it wouldn't have worked for him just to pretend that he no longer distrusted people—he had a strong belief, ingrained in his unconscious, that people weren't to be trusted! And it wasn't that his model was inaccurate—in fact, the way he lived his life, based on his context, tended to attract a fair number of untrustworthy people—it was that his model was *not effective* at getting him the quality of life he wanted. So he had some thinking to do.

After some brainstorming, Tony came up with not one but *three* new points of view he could take that helped him overcome his old, self-sabotaging attitude of distrust:

1. Trust is important in a good relationship, and I want a good relationship, so it's worth taking the risk.
2. If I trust people, they'll tend to live up to that trust (he knew that was true for himself).
3. It's scary to start trusting people, but it couldn't turn out any worse than the way my life is now!

Tony realized he had a choice. Rather than thinking his beliefs were his beliefs for all time, and that's just the way he was, he realized he could choose his beliefs. And even though he didn't know how to erase his old beliefs about trust instantaneously, he did come up with some new attitudes in favor of trust he could believe in.

He didn't "have to" believe trusting people was harmful. Instead, *he chose points of view that supported what was important to him*—a good relationship, a good job, more money. Rather than letting his context run him, he chose his own context. He made what was most important to him in life *really be* the most important thing in his life—more important than hanging on to some beliefs and points of view that must have felt like old friends by now.

Gradually, Tony's context filter started to let through opportunities for some of the things he was now clear were important to him. When a job offer came along, Tony initially reacted with his old fears and attitudes, but then remembered his three new points of view about trust and accepted in spite of the fear. He started being more trusting in his relationships, and they improved too. It took work, was scary, and felt uncomfortable, but Tony was willing to shift his model of life did what it took to get what was most important to him. And of course he lived happily ever after.

People get so attached to their points of view. Do you know people who would rather be right than happy? When it becomes clear that the way you're looking at a situation is interfering with what you want out of life—find other ways to look at it.

> To enjoy life to its fullest, choose points of view that support you in living the life you want.

BEING PRINCIPLED, OR BEING STUBBORN?

Most people have some positions or beliefs that they would never consider budging from. People have morals, boundaries—principles that are deeply rooted. These are principles you wouldn't violate even if it meant a better chance at getting something important: the ends would not justify the means. Violating these principles would not just feel uncomfortable, it would feel *wrong*. I'm not recommending you violate any of these principles.

What I *am* recommending is you consider any other position, attitude, point of view, or belief fair game if it's getting in the way of what is most important to you. It's admirable to be stubborn when it comes to standing up for those core, bedrock principles. But when you're stubborn about anything else, and you're letting that get in the way of something more important to you, all you're doing is sabotaging your own life. Don't make consistency more important than your own life! It's OK to look at something from one point of view today and from a different one tomorrow!

Oh, by the way: I guess the Sun doesn't actually set in the west—turns out it stays relatively still while the Earth rotates toward the east. Truth!

5

♦

Fear and Purpose

Tell us your phobias and we will tell you what you are afraid of.

—*Robert Benchley*

Life is a series of choices. Most choices we make unconsciously; some consciously. In either case, we make choices based on the sum total of all our beliefs, attitudes, opinions, remembered experiences, and so on—our context.

Many of the little pieces of our context have to do with fear. Each time something dangerous or painful happens—say my Seventh-Grade math teacher yells at me after I speak out in class without waiting to be called on—a little red flag gets planted in my unconscious around that subject, causing me to feel fear if I approach something similar to that again. Later, I get an icy stare from another teacher, also for speaking out of turn. Soon, my intelligence kicks in and starts noticing patterns—all unconsciously, still. Now I have a big red sign warning me against that whole kind of behavior—I become afraid to be too visible in class. My unconscious is protecting me. Thanks, unconscious!

The trouble is, after going through a few years of this, I'm done with school, and now I want to publish books, give workshops and speak in front of large groups. All of a sudden these warning signals are working against me—people are paying to listen to me speak, yet my context is full of big red signs warning me not to be too visible. How likely is my Seventh-Grade math teacher to yell at me now, even if Mr. Reed makes it to one of my workshops? Not very, I hope. But it takes work to convince my unconscious of that!

Fortunately, since I had an extremely strong commitment to do this kind of work, I was willing to work through the fears and establish new patterns. I was clear about my purpose in the situation, and so I was willing to move through my fears.

Next time you're in the self-help section of your favorite bookstore, notice all the books about fear. Unwanted or irrational fear is a big issue for people today. But why is that? Why do we have unwanted fears? It doesn't make sense, does it?

People spend their whole lives trying to find answers to "why" questions like that, and the answer often doesn't yield much benefit other than to satisfy our curiosity. Perhaps as animals evolved, the ones that remembered to be afraid of dangerous things for a long time tended to survive and reproduce better, and so that characteristic became common in animals as well as people. In our world today, however, our environment changes so fast that remembering fears from the past is usually not helping anything. In particular, the fears we had as relatively powerless children and that hold us back as adults are often completely unwarranted now that we are relatively powerful grown-ups.

Making fear the most important thing in life is a survival strategy. The trouble is, most of us have survival pretty well handled most of the time. Unless you are often in physical danger, there's no need to make fear, which is designed to protect us from physical danger, the most important thing in your life. If you want your life to be about more than survival—if you have any desire to do more with your life than just make it through—then you must make something else more important than fear.

> Fear will rule your life unless you make something else more important.

Without a sense of purpose to life, a sense of what is truly most important to us, we become like the ball in a pinball machine, bouncing away from fear after fear. When we have a clear purpose, we may feel afraid or encounter obstacles, but we will do what it takes to move through the fear and solve the problems in front of us.

Without being clear about a purpose, we tend to bounce around from fear to fear as if we were the ball in a pinball machine.

PURPOSE

The word "purpose" means many things. When I talk about being "on purpose," I mean consciously making choices, speaking, and acting in accordance with what is most important to you, rather than waiting for things to happen to you and reacting when they do. You can have a mini-purpose to a particular situation, or an overall life purpose.

For instance, if I have a mini-purpose to have a high-paying job, and from that mini-purpose create a goal of getting a raise within six months, I would take steps toward that goal: gather materials to show my boss why it would be in his or her best interest to raise my salary; set up a support network of friends to bounce ideas off of and keep me focused; make an appointment to pop the question; and so on.

Without being clear on that mini-purpose, I would be much less likely to succeed: chances are, I would not gather supporting materials or build a support network because it would be too much work; not make an appointment because it would be too scary; and not ask directly for a raise because I would fear rejection.

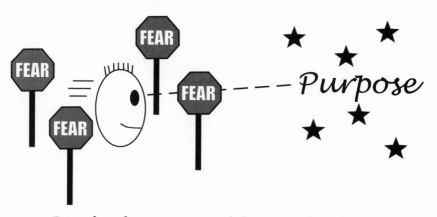

Being clear about your purpose helps you get through fears.

My wife Dana and I share a clear mini-purpose in our marriage to have a great relationship—including mutual love, support, respect, and understanding. Being clear about what is most important to us helps us move through the fears that come up in any intimate relationship.

When we fight, we are (eventually) likely to focus on how to heal the disagreement rather than think about leaving the relationship out of fear that it's not a safe place. We are more likely to look for ways to support each other, and accept each other's support, than to fear being taken advantage of and have a power struggle.

We are more likely to focus on respecting each other rather than punishing each other as a reaction to our fear of being hurt—and justifying why the other one deserves it. We tend to be honest with each other about our feelings and desires rather than giving in to our fear of saying something we think may upset the other one.

All this happens because our relationship is based on *purpose*. What's the difference?

When you have a purpose, you *cause* things to happen in your life. When you don't, your life feels more like the *effect* of things happening to you.

With a purpose, you steer your life in a direction you consciously choose; without it, you tend to be carried about in no particular direction by the currents of life. Now, there's nothing *wrong* with letting yourself be blown around by the winds of fate—it just doesn't help you get more of what's most important to you. So if you're clear about what that is, why not make it your purpose to get more of it? And if you're not clear, why not get clear?

PURPOSE VERSUS GOAL

When I first came across this idea of being clear about my purpose in each situation, I confused the word "purpose" with the word "goal." The difference is subtle: having a goal will also help you move through fear; achieving a goal can also help you focus your life on what is truly most important to you; visualizing a goal can help keep you on track and keep you from bouncing around at random, away from various scary things.

The difference is this: a goal has an end; a purpose is ongoing. At work, goals might include "make $50,000 a year," "get promoted to Group Manager," and "complete project on schedule." But a *purpose* for working might include "enjoy my job," "support family comfortably," and "be known to myself and others as a reliable person who does an excellent job and keeps his agreements."

Mini-Purpose	Goals
Enjoy my job.	Get assigned to my first-choice project.
	Find or recruit a group of people I enjoy having lunch with.
	Handle to-do list by completing or scheduling all items.
Support family comfortably.	Get salary raised to $50,000 per year within five years.
	Persuade management to include child care in benefit package.
Be respected and admired for doing superior work.	Complete project on schedule.
	Get promoted to Group Manager.
	Speak up and contribute in next month's design meeting rather than avoid conflict.
Have a great marriage	Stay married as long as we both shall live.
	Save $10,000 in next five years for down-payment on house.
	Do whatever it takes to resolve toilet-seat issue.

See the difference? Once a goal is achieved, it's over. But all the components of a purpose are continuing experiences that don't have a particular deadline or ending. They are threads that, when woven together, form a particular texture of life that you find appealing.

If you have several different arenas in which you spend significant portions of your time—for instance, a job, a family, and a volunteer group—you may want to have a different mini-purpose for each arena reflecting the different texture of experience you want to have in each place.

If you're wondering about how to come up with these mini-purposes, or if you're a person who is comfortable with the idea of goals, but don't quite identify yet with how a purpose is different or what it would get you, it helps to have an overall sense of what is most important to you in your whole life.

And if you are not yet clear about *that*, I would suggest that you make this your highest priority: having the richest, fullest, most meaningful, worthwhile life possible. With that in mind, you can extract these mini-purposes for each area of your life so that they all add up to a life that maximizes everything you consider to be most important. By your own standards.

6

◆

That's Life!

I went to the woods because I wished to live deliberately, to front only the essential facts of life, and see if I could not learn what it had to teach, and not, when I came to die, discover that I had not lived.

—*Henry David Thoreau*

Human consciousness is an incredible, wonderful gift. The more people I meet, the more I realize we are unique, good, amazing beings, each of us with a unique gift to bring to the world, each of us with our own light to shine. It's just that sometimes we get a little bit bogged down in this big distraction known as reality.

It reminds me of what archaeologists find when they dig through the ruins of ancient civilizations: layer upon layer of the trash thrown away by each of the previous groups of people who've lived there. I have an image of our brains burdened by layer upon layer of trashy, discarded attitudes and opinions from past years and generations, all telling us different ways we "should" live life. This crushing burden can come crashing down on us when we do practically anything—the advice is all so conflicting, it's always possible to catch ourselves violating some piece of it, if that's what we're afraid of.

Ultimately, you're going to live your life the way you live your life: with seriousness or frivolity; with a sense of purpose or not; with passion or apathy. You are the only one who gets to decide. I think a lot of us go on year after year, putting off our dreams, waiting for something to happen, settling for less than what we want "temporarily," then for longer, and longer, as if someone were going to come to us when it gets bad enough and say, "Hey, enough is enough! It's your turn now! Time to make some changes!" If that's what you were waiting for, then I'll say it now. Or better yet, say it to yourself.

"You mean that was life? But no one told me I could start!"

I hope that you, in reading this book, will at the very least make a conscious choice about what you want your life to be about. It is our blessing and our curse that we have the ability to choose. Are you going to choose to have the richest, fullest life possible? Or are you going to shove these ideas into a corner of your attic, maybe the same corner where you have stuffed your dreams, and say maybe you'll think about it later, when you have more time, or money, or energy, or . . . ?

I want you to live a life of fulfillment rather than a life of survival. That means identifying what is truly most important in your life—what is worthwhile, good, right, passionate, or however *you* define what makes life worth living—and making your life be about that instead of about trying to make sense and consistency of all the external messages telling you how to live your life, bouncing from fear to fear, or simply coasting on idle.

You can overcome whatever obstacles you think you have inherited from your genes, lack of ability, or current circumstances. You can.

You can rely on your own judgment about what is best for you, what is most important to you, what your contribution is to the world, and what you want your life to be about. You can.

You can work towards having the richest, fullest life possible, by your own standards. You can.

Why not make the commitment to start now?

PART II

◆

LIBERTY

7

◆

Peace and Freedom

We hold these truths to be self-evident; that all men are created equal; that they are endowed by their creator with certain unalienable rights; that among these rights are life, liberty, and the pursuit of happiness.
—Declaration of Independence

If you read books written by people who feel they've made huge breakthroughs in their quality of life—who believe, some of them, that they have found the *secret* of life—one common theme is "inner peace." I'm going to stay away from the transcendental, metaphysical, and other profound implications of inner peace, and simply focus on one fact: whatever you want to accomplish in your life, you've got a lot more energy to devote to it if you don't have a lot of quacking ducks nibbling at your toes all day and all night.

This section, *Liberty,* deals with freeing yourself from the stuff you don't want in your life. I'm not sure if the authors of the Declaration of Independence deliberately listed *life, liberty, and the pursuit of happiness* in that order because they believed they had to be achieved in that order, but if they didn't, then I'll say it now.

Since you are reading these words now and not fighting off alligators or some such menace, I trust you have the *life* part pretty much under control for the time being. Great! You're a third of the way there! Congratulations.

The final section, *The Pursuit of Happiness,* talks about what it would take for you to have the greatest, most fulfilling, meaningful, worthwhile life possible, by your own standards. In this section, I'm going to tell you everything I know about personal *liberty:* how to free yourself from whatever is preventing you from having the best life you can imagine. We do this part first, before the fun part, because it's just too hard to hear the birds of paradise singing songs of serenity when you've got the constant clamor of the ducks of despair quacking quacks of crisis.

As you read through this section, please remember one very important thing: no one can keep you from having the liberty, peace, and freedom I'm talking about here. This is a subject between you and you. I want you to liberate yourself from stress, be at peace with yourself, and have the freedom to devote your life to whatever is most important to you. The main concept underlying this section is *self-acceptance.*

Whenever I use a psycho-pop buzzword, I like to say what I really mean, just because I know how my eyes start to glaze over whenever I read one of them. Accepting yourself means understanding who you are, and how your life currently stands, without fighting or resisting that knowledge. It does *not* mean you can't want to change, improve, or grow. It does *not* mean you're settling for less than you deserve, or giving up on your dreams. It does *not* mean you are abandoning your morality, integrity, or values. Absolutely not!

This is almost a paradox, but people really work this way:

> It is difficult to have real change, improvement, or growth in your life while you are resisting or fighting the reality of who you are and how your life stands right now.

Any growth in your life, like it or not, is going to build on who you are right now. We don't get to start over. So you might as well accept yourself as you are now and go from there.

WHO IS THIS FOR?

I chuckle as I look over these last words, thinking how much I would have resisted them had I read them ten years ago. It's not that I would have disagreed with them, but I would have read them, paused for a second or two in thought, said to myself, "OK, I accept myself," and toyed with the idea of skipping ahead to the fun section on the pursuit of happiness. I *would not have accepted* the notion that I had areas where I *did not accept* myself.

So I assume my target audience here, people who are already successful in one or more areas of their life, may have similar concerns. Let me point out that I'm not attempting to criticize you for lack of self-acceptance, or even say that it's "bad" or "wrong" not to accept yourself. As I said before, I was tremendously successful, and in my mother's view a very nice person, before I ever ran into any of this personal-growth stuff. But, especially if you're a good problem-solver or crisis-handler like me, the growth comes in areas where you don't see problems or crises.

I'm not saying your life's a disaster (if it is, you'd better hurry up and keep reading). But I do think it's easy to fill life with little problems, crises, and obligations, and before you know it, you're in a state of equilibrium between OK and Crisis, leaving very little time for Fantastic and Fulfilling. This book is about shifting the equilibrium to be past OK and on towards Fantastic.

If the connection between self-acceptance and having a more fulfilling life is not yet clear, or if you're a very, very curious person who is still wondering if you have complete self-acceptance already and would it be OK to skip to page 147, let me give my best shot at a quick answer. If there are areas where you don't fully accept yourself, it can show up as stress, anxiety, depression, or insomnia; as guilt, anger, or resentment; or as being often upset by the actions of other people or by the way the world is. If you have a fair amount of any of those (you see why I am assuming that this would be of interest to most people?) you have a lot to gain by reading this section.

Fulfillment

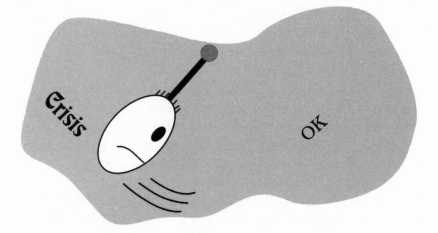

Our lives can become an equilibrium between OK and Crisis, leaving Fulfillment off in the distance, seemingly unreachable.

> You may have lots of self-acceptance already. If you do, you have even more to gain by finding those areas where it's missing.

SELF-ESTEEM

The other nice side-effect of increasing your self-acceptance is that it tends to automatically increase your *self-esteem*, or how good you feel about yourself. While that's certainly desirable just for its own sake, I've heard people say over and over again that when they feel better about themselves, *they also feel better about all of the other relationships in their lives.*

Do you have some days when you feel so good nothing anyone does can bother you? Do you have other days when you're so cranky nobody had better even look at you the wrong way? That's the principle I'm talking about—if you feel better about yourself overall, life's other problems become that much easier to handle.

I remember a time when my self-esteem was truly at a lifetime low. There was one guy at work who bugged me so much, I couldn't even stand to be in the same room with him. I couldn't even stand to look at him! In fact, just the fact that he was alive bothered me. I decided I was a "victim of the rat-race"—that I just couldn't take working with people like that any longer—and quit my job to relieve the stress. In fact, I quit everything in my life: besides leaving my job, I sold my car, sold my house, moved back to the East Coast, broke my engagement, and grew a beard.

A funny thing happened, though. After the novelty wore off—a couple of months—I began to hate my new job almost as much as my old job. And I began to realize that Boston wasn't as great a place to live as I thought it would be. And my new condo had all kinds of problems, just like my old house. And my new car had a new set of problems. And all the women I met had some fatal flaw. And the beard itched.

Although all those things back at my old job really did bug me, and I really did have a lot of stress, my mistake was in thinking I could cure it by replacing all those things with new ones. Those greener pastures *really did* look greener, thanks to my context. I could taste how green they were! But the way I felt about myself, it was no wonder *anyplace else* looked like a greener pasture.

Self-acceptance and self-esteem are like the water that floats the boat. You can have a relationship on the rocks or a job stuck on a sand bar, and increasing your self-esteem will raise the water level so everything gets lifted up simultaneously. Feeling better about yourself naturally causes you to feel better about everything else in your life.

> The quality of your relationships has a lot to do with your own self-acceptance and self-esteem. Raising them tends to automatically raise the quality of your relationships.

So if you have a job or relationship that's going nowhere, or just not working—before you learn a very expensive lesson about greener pastures, check in honestly with yourself and see if you really feel good about who you are as a person. Because if you're down on yourself, that's not a good time to make decisions about jobs or relationships. The ones you're in all look bad, and the ones you're not in all look better. That's the time to work on accepting yourself for who you are, which will automatically improve the quality of *all* parts of your life.

I don't think it's possible for your level of self-esteem to be any greater than your level of self-acceptance. If there are parts of yourself you don't accept, what are you telling yourself? "Those parts of me are bad," "Only a terrible person would be like that," "I wish I were someone else"? How high can your self-esteem be when you are telling yourself things like that? You've got to accept *all* of you to have the best life you can.

HOW DO YOU DO IT?

Increasing self-acceptance is not simply a matter of flipping a switch. We are extremely clever, we human beings, and often sabotage our own best interests with our cleverness. In particular, we often set up all kinds of behavior patterns and thought processes that keep us right smack where we are today, and that includes keeping us at our current level of self-knowledge.

While reading this, if you're thinking thoughts like "I don't have any work to do," "Come on—everybody in my line of work has lots of stress," "This stuff would be great for my Aunt Zelda, but I don't think I need it," or "I'm getting bored with this drivel. I wonder what's on TV?" you might be experiencing self-sabotaging thought patterns first hand. Just read the whole book; it's not that long.

The things I talk about in this section are not physically difficult to do. It's a matter of overcoming inertia, of breaking some patterns of behavior and establishing some new ones. It takes energy, though, to do that, so it's got to be worth your while. What it would mean to you to get more of whatever is most important to you in your life, or to get rid of the big negatives?

Do you have a dream? Do you long to do something important with your life, to make a difference in the world? Are you committed to spending your life doing what is most important to you, no matter what it takes? If you are, focusing on your dream will make it easier to get over the speed bumps of fear or discomfort that are keeping you where you are now.

If you're not committed to having the most fulfilling, meaningful, worthwhile life possible, or if you're unsure, it's OK just to read this book and learn what I'm talking about without making a commitment—that's why I wrote the book. But if you are committed to having a great life, or if this is your second (or third . . . ?) time through the book—please, please, please: *really do it!* Letting your eyes float over the words is not sufficient to get what you want out of life! Please be true to yourself and do what it takes to have a great life.

8

◆

Honesty

This above all: to thine own self be true.
—William Shakespeare

While I recommend honesty in general—after all, it *is* the best policy—what I'm talking about in this chapter is being honest with yourself. That is, no matter how good you are at feeding people lines, at squirming your way out of situations with "creative" explanations, or at impressing people with your image of total perfection—don't lie to yourself.

If you're reading this book because you want to get somewhere in your life, somewhere other than where you are today, please realize that when you take a trip, knowing the destination is not enough to get you there: you also have to know where you are starting from. All the maps in the world won't help you get anywhere unless you know where you are now. If I live in Cleveland and I want to go to Hawaii, it won't do me any good to book a flight from New York City, even if I wish I were living there. The flight has to start in Cleveland if I want to be on it.

So just between you and me, for the duration of this book, set your image aside. If someone wants to know why you're reading this book, and you want to tell them you're just looking for some advice to give your friends on how they can break some of their bad habits—fine. Just tell the truth to yourself.

To help you get an accurate picture of where you are right now, I'm going to go through several areas in which people tend to distort reality for whatever reason. As you read along, you'll get the most benefit by thinking about how this applies to you, and how cleaning up any distortions or myths you have about yourself might help you get closer to what you want out of life.

ABILITY (AND LACK OF IT)

I'm going to start with what I feel is the most destructive single lie that people tell themselves: the myth that "I can't."

While there are obviously some things we physically cannot do—be in two places at once, lift a 16-ton weight, run a mile in ten seconds—usually when people say "I can't," they really mean something else. From now on, every time you are about to say "I can't," think about what you really mean. Often it's a "polite" way of saying that something is simply not important enough to you right now, given your priorities.

I'm not suggesting you start being rude to people, answering birthday-party invitations with "No dice, buddy! You're just not a priority!" I personally avoid the use of "I can't" when I'm not talking about physical limitations, even in conversations with other people, just to keep in practice; but the important thing here is that you be honest in your conversations with *yourself*.

If you're like me, as soon as you make a habit of saying or thinking what you really mean instead of "I can't," you'll find yourself much more conscious of what is most important to you and what your priorities are. If you're declining to do someone a favor because of a previous commitment, then it's not that you "can't" drive him to the airport, it's that it's important to you to keep your previous commitment. The underlying belief here that I'd like to strengthen in you is this:

> I *can do* just about anything if I choose to make it a high enough priority and devote enough time, money, and energy to it.

Sometimes people say "I can't" because they believe there are some things they would "have to" do, if it weren't for the fact that "I can't." Wow—double self-deceit! Suppose I say to myself, "I can't" work on my book this afternoon because "I have to" go pick up the car from the repair shop. Let's go through it step by step. First, as we know, I *can* work on my book this afternoon if it's important enough to me. The question is, what's more important to me, working on my book, or picking up my car?

Well, obviously, working on my book: this is my dream, my passion in life, a very high priority, while frankly I have little interest in picking up the car. So what about this "have to" business? As we saw in the chapter on *Choices,* "I have to" really means *I choose to* when I consider the negative consequences of not doing it. Aha! So I finally have this mess untangled, this mess caused by my sleazy use of "can't" and "have to" to avoid looking at reality. The reality is, I have a choice: which is a higher priority, working on my book, or picking up my car, considering the negative consequences if I don't pick it up?

What began as frustrating and stressful gets quite a bit clearer when, instead of muddying the situation by using the self-limiting language "can't" and "have to," I put the thing in terms of my real choices and priorities. In fact, looking at the problem that way opens the door for creative solutions: can I get someone else to pick up the car for me? Can I dictate my book into a tape recorder while I go get the car? I'm only hurting myself by lying to myself: by using self-limiting language, I'm steering myself away from the best solution to the problem.

> Instead of saying or thinking "I can't," figure out what you really mean. For most things, you really can if you're willing to make them a high enough priority.

So why do we use self-limiting language? Beats me. All I can say (or all I *choose to* say at this point, given my current thoughts on the subject) is there are plenty of things we do that aren't in our best interest. There are thoughts, modes of behavior, patterns, myths, and general confusion floating around that don't particularly do us any good. We tend to copy what we see other people doing. When we talk about people learning by *osmosis*—picking up a skill or knowledge without formally being taught—they likely are copying behaviors, modes of thought, or whatever is necessary to "pick up" the skill. Just make sure the things you pick up are things you want!

REASONS, EXCUSES, AND JUSTIFICATIONS

As if it weren't destructive enough to lie to ourselves about something as basic as our ability—telling ourselves we can't when we perfectly well can if we just allocate the resources—the game goes on to the next level. Here's the dialog, one we're trained to recite practically from the first moment we can speak:

"Will you do A?" *(fearful hush comes over the audience)*
"I can't." *(applause!)*

"Why not?" *(anticipation builds to the point of frenzy)*
"Because B!" *(standing ovation with shouts of "Bravo!")*

After digging our own grave by lying to ourselves about our ability, the next thing we do is start reinforcing it with cement by layering excuses on top of it. If we get good enough at it, we start believing them ourselves! Do other people believe them? Probably not. Are there people you know who always have good excuses for everything? Regardless of the quality of the excuse, the reality is the thing is not getting done; yet there are other people who succeed in doing it. No matter how good the excuse, the result is still the result.

Excuses, reasons, justifications—they're like evidence at a trial, exhibits for the defense supporting your decisions or actions as if the simple truth that you made the best decision you could at the time

"Your honor, the defense presents excuse #536 for not having a great life."

were not enough. "I quit my job because the boss was too domineering." "I want to take a vacation because I haven't had one in six months." Most likely, the decision to quit had other factors besides the boss's personality; maybe six months from now you'll be absorbed in your project at work and not want to take a vacation. Many decisions are intuitive, and based on the entirety of your life and who you are as a human being. You're not required to give reasons or justifications for everything you do.

> When you make excuses, or defend your decisions with reasons or justifications, return your focus to what is most important to you. If you are committed to what is most important to you, you don't need reasons or excuses.

KEEPING AGREEMENTS

The place where reasons, excuses, and justifications flourish, and I think the place where they are most self-destructive to the quality of life we desire, is when we use them to justify breaking agreements.

If I break an agreement, it's broken. If I tell my copy editor I'm going to have this chapter done by Thursday, and Thursday passes, and it isn't done, the agreement is broken. No matter what my reasons, how good my excuses, or how well I justify it, I broke the agreement. Now, if I only do this once, my editor isn't going to fly off the handle and give up on me, whether I have a good excuse or not. But if the same thing happens every week, no matter how good my excuses are, any sane editor is, at the very least, going to find some other work to do on Thursdays rather than wait around for my manuscript.

At this point in my life, I sometimes find myself astounded that people even ask for excuses when someone breaks an agreement with them. I rarely do any more; I just assume the person in question has made a choice in accordance with his or her priorities. Something came up that was more important to that person than keeping our agreement. I had one teacher in high school whose assignments were due when they were due; he granted no extensions and accepted no excuses, even for illness. Most of the class, myself included, thought this was grossly unfair, and at one point we had the whole PTA harassing this poor guy for damaging our potential college admissions by not giving a perfect grade to someone who missed an assignment with a "good excuse."

What was the teacher's point? As I look back, I think I missed a valuable lesson. In life, no matter how good your excuse is, your result is still your result. If you have the best excuses in the world for not sending out those job resumes—well, you still don't have a job. If you have complete justification for putting off those decisions about how to invest your money—well, you still haven't invested your money. If you have all the reasons in the world for not joining a health club, meeting potential mates, eating a healthy diet, or getting clear on what you want your life to be about—guess what? You can sell those excuses to everyone in the world, including yourself, and your results are still your results.

Do you ever say you're "too tired" to do something? Are you really *physically* too tired? If Ed MacMahon were at the door with a check for $10 million would you be too tired to answer the door? How about "too old" or "too young"? There are very few things people are *really* too old for; having children is one, and even that can be handled if you plan ahead.

Any excuse of the form "I don't have enough time/money/ energy" is just another self-deceit: time, money, and energy are resources you can allocate according to your priorities. What's most important to you? If you're using an "I don't have enough ..." excuse, but you're spending time, money, or energy on something less important to you, you're fooling yourself.

My point is *not* that it's morally wrong to make excuses, or that you should cleanse yourself of this type of thinking to make yourself a better person. Not at all. But when you start buying into your own excuses, you are not doing yourself a favor. You're creating a layer of confusion between you and what's most important to you in life. If you want to go ahead and keep using excuses with other people, that's fine—although I stopped doing that when I began to realize that other people saw through them as well as I did. But be true to yourself.

From now on, every time you catch yourself making an excuse to yourself, do a reality check. Instead of saying, "I'm too tired to cook tonight," figure out what you really mean. Do you mean having the experience of relaxing tonight or the experience of eating a pepperoni pizza is more important than saving money and eating a healthy meal? If that's true, it's fine with me: be honest—not to beat yourself up about it, but just to live in reality. You need to know where you are in order to get where you want to go.

TRUSTING YOURSELF

There's something even more valuable about being honest with yourself than the important benefit of knowing where you stand today, and that's the value you get out of *trusting yourself.*

The whole point of this book is to help you live the most worthwhile, meaningful, fulfilling life possible. Trusting yourself would be a great tool towards that, don't you think? Wouldn't it be great to know you could make a commitment to yourself to devote your life to those things that are most important to you, and know you would keep that commitment?

When I was a kid, I used to fib a lot. I vividly remember one evening, though, when my brother and I both denied having done something or other, and my father believed my brother, but not me. I took it hard, especially so because my parents had always treated us fairly and equally. So I wailed to my dad that it wasn't fair, why did he believe Bobby and not me? That day, I heard some of the most painful and useful feedback of my life. My father told me, straight out, that he didn't trust me, as I had a reputation for lying, while my brother didn't.

Ouch! I remember my throat tightening. It was a long time ago, but I still remember being just about to launch into a manipulative crying session, and then not doing it. Something about the plain, non-judgmental way my father laid it out for me helped me break out of that pattern and think about who I wanted to be as contrasted with who I was. Because he was right! Although I had never thought about it consciously, I knew that I was a liar—or at least a fibber, but in any case I had ruined my reputation to the point where my own father didn't believe me.

I asked my father what it would take to restore my reputation, and he replied I would have to tell only the truth. For how long? I asked. Without making it sound like punishment, he honestly said he thought it would have to be at least two years. Now, two years is an awful long time to a 13-year-old kid! But what were the alternatives? Since that day, I have taken great pains to tell the truth and to keep my word to other people. For many years, if I ever failed to keep my word, I felt a lot of pain, beat myself up, replayed the situation over and over, trying to figure out what went wrong, and resolved anew to be better at keeping my word.

But even with that lesson, which permanently changed the way I valued my word with other people, it never occurred to me that there might be value in keeping my word with *myself.*

> If you want to trust yourself, which is a key part of self-acceptance, you've simply got to keep your word with yourself.

Some people motivate themselves by keeping themselves in a permanent state of having broken agreements with themselves hanging over their heads. This is called *procrastination.* For obvious reasons, it tends to produce stress. Because handling my procrastination was the biggest single change I made in my life to increase my peace and allow room for some of the good stuff, I have devoted a whole chapter to it.

9

◆

Procrastination

Time is the great teacher, but unfortunately it kills all of its students.

—Hector Berlioz

If procrastination were just a matter of being lazy, I wouldn't have much problem with it. Lazy people have many strengths, among them an amazing talent for finding the easiest, most effortless way to do things. If procrastination were just laziness, overcoming it

79

would simply be a matter of accepting that I was being lazy: I could either live with that, or decide that something else was more important to me and do that instead.

But in fact, many people procrastinate without being lazy at all. My favorite way to avoid doing important things was to do the third, fourth, or fifth most important thing on my priority list. Numbers one and two would never get done. No, procrastination is a clever way we sabotage ourselves by keeping our stress level just high enough to make us miserable. I don't know how many times I spent days or weeks full of fear and anxiety about something hanging over my head, only to complete it, or at least get over the hump, in a few minutes or hours. What a waste! Not only didn't I get the thing done, but I spent all that time feeling bad! Each undone task we procrastinate hangs around our neck like a weight and, whether we are conscious of it or not, drains our energy. When we procrastinate, we lose three times: the thing doesn't get done, we carry around the weight or bad feeling about not having done it, and the stress and energy drain keeps us from directing our attention to what's most important to us.

I really want to sell you on getting rid of the procrastination in your life. Do you identify with me when I talk about each undone item being like a little weight, adding a little stress, hurting a little in the pit of your stomach, adding a little worry or anxiety? Do you go through the day with thoughts of undones creeping into your head only to be quickly shoved out? Do you lie awake at night running through lists of unfinished business? Then you have a huge, tremendous, enormous amount to gain by breaking your pattern. Procrastination is curable.

I used to have to-do lists of my to-do lists. I used to torture myself by visualizing the things I had hanging over my head. I tortured myself lying awake at night, and then again first thing in the morning as I woke. And I had a lot of undones! When I decided to get serious about cleaning up my act, I spent over a week, nonstop, tying up dozens of loose ends that I had left dangling over the years. And you can bet I'm much more conscious now about what I agree to—either with others, or with myself.

THE CURE

It is not difficult to cure procrastination. It doesn't involve anything deep, profound, or metaphysical. You don't even have to know your purpose in life. You just have to do it. However, for advanced procrastinators such as I was, I have compiled some advanced methods for dividing and conquering your undones. Remember, we're doing this to increase self-trust, get more energy, feel better, and create a foundation for Part III of this book: having the greatest, most fulfilling life possible. *Don't skip this part!*

> If you keep all that stuff hanging over your head, it's just a built-in excuse not to do what's most important to you.

It'll always be "when I get out from under this load" or "when I get my life in a little less chaos" or "when I'm not so busy." Without *consciously* committing to handle our undones, and keep them handled, we tend to keep ourselves stuck in an equilibrium of as much stress as we can handle. Yuck! I did that for a long time and, believe me, I'm not going back!

So here's how to do it. If you don't trust me, or you are the rare person who actually does read the entire instruction booklet before plugging in the toaster, go ahead and absorb the information now. *But then go back and really do it!* Just try it! When it comes to handling your undones, the gain far outweighs the pain.

You will be making three lists, so you'll need at least three sheets of paper (or more if you're like me) and a pen. If you're the kind of person who shudders at the thought of making lists, it's OK to get creative and make this fun—but please use something relatively permanent, like ink and paper or a computer, rather than a blackboard, sand on a beach, or a cake-decorating kit. You will also need your date book, calendar, or scheduling program.

At the top of one sheet of paper, write "Undones." At the top of the second, write "Excuses." And at the top of the third, write "Avoiders." I'll explain how to use each of these lists in a moment.

S T E P   1 :   W R I T E   I T   D O W N

Ready? This part doesn't even involve doing anything hard. I want you to free up the mental energy you spend juggling these undones into and out of your consciousness. So on your sheet of paper entitled "Undones," write down all the things you're supposed to do that you consider undone. These are only the energy-drainers, the things you feel like you have to do (but haven't), the ones that knot your stomach or keep you awake at night. *Don't* include your dreams, career goals, relationship fantasies, or that kind of thing; we're saving that for the fun section. This is just the hard stuff.

If you have ongoing projects in which you honestly are making current progress, you are clear about and have scheduled your next step, and you genuinely feel they are "handled," not "undone," don't put those on the list. You're in good shape with those already.

It's OK if it takes a while, but stop when you've written everything that comes to mind—you don't have to rack your brain. Chances are, when you handle a few of these, you'll free up space for some new ones; from now on, whenever a new undone pops into your head, add it to your list. The list does not have to be perfect; the idea is just to transfer the tasks from your mental juggling act to the main tent, thus freeing up your mind for more interesting things. You can also stop beating yourself up now for having put these things off: you are right now, at this very moment, in the process of handling them. Congratulations!

As you make your list, in addition to chores, assignments, and tasks that need to be done, write down undones involving people you need to talk to, issues that need to be resolved, or other energy-draining loose ends involving communicating with other people. If you're not sure whether you're really going to do something, write it down anyway; you'll have a chance to cross it off later. Just get them out from their hiding places.

During this process, you have an excellent opportunity to become conscious of some of the ways you sabotage your own success. (Don't worry—you don't have to actually *do* any of your undones yet.) On the sheet of paper entitled "Excuses," write down all the excuses, justifications, and reasons why not that pop into your head as you contemplate doing any or all of the undones. This can be an ongoing list, and I promise not to hold it against you. The purpose of the list of excuses is not to prove what a terrible human being you are, but simply to give yourself some ammunition against the sabotage.

By the way, the idea is to write them down *instead of using them!* Most people have favorite excuses and use the same ones for lots of different things, so this list can help you raise a red flag if you ever start focusing on excuses instead of what's most important to you.

"I'll just think about it now, and write it down later . . ."

We might as well start the third list now, entitled "Avoiders." No, this is not a list of people you want to avoid, although you may feel free to add unresolved relationship issues with them to your "Undones" list. This list is going to list your favorite *activities* you do *while you procrastinate*. It is a list of what you tend to do while you are *avoiding* doing something more important.

Now, these things don't have to be intrinsically bad activities— sleeping, talking on the phone, cleaning house, and so on are all perfectly fine things to be doing. The point, once again, is to *become aware* of your favorite ways to avoid, so when you find yourself doing them you can raise a red flag and ask yourself if that particular activity is most important to you right now. For activities such as sleeping, the answer will be "yes" sometimes—just be honest.

Once again, the point here is *not* to give yourself a big club to clobber yourself with. Nothing you put on these lists can be used against you! Remember, we're doing this to *increase* self-acceptance, not decrease it. If you do find yourself getting down on yourself for using excuses or avoiding, I recommend adopting a position of healthy curiosity: "Huh! Isn't that interesting! I keep wanting to call Aunt Zelda every time I have several hours available to work on my book. And I don't even like talking to her! I wonder what I'm avoiding?" Please be nice to yourself. You're doing yourself a big favor by becoming conscious of your excuses and avoiders—it's not fair to punish yourself for it!

The "Excuses" and "Avoiders" lists don't have to be complete right now—just add to them whenever one comes up. So if you haven't started already, go ahead and start making your three lists. When you've written down all the undones that come to mind, remembering that you can add more later, go on to the next step.

STEP 2: CLASSIFY IT

There are only two ways to get rid of an undone: you can do it, or you can decide you are never, ever going to do it. "Maybe" doesn't count—that's what got you into this mess. Now, when I say "do it," I don't necessarily mean you have to finish it today—just get it to the point where you're satisfied it's being handled. There's a huge difference between something you've been avoiding that's hanging over your head and something that you've started, and you're currently working on, but just isn't done yet. Our goal is to take everything on that list, and everything that will ever get added to that list, and either get it to the point where we're making current progress on it, or get rid of it forever. Keep that list short! Undones are hazardous to your health!

So here we go. Are you excited? You are actually going to feel better and have lots more of yourself available to do the fun stuff that you want to do with your life! Ready?

Go!

If you're ready, go through each item on your list. Don't skip any! For each item, decide whether you are committed to doing it, or whether you are giving yourself permission to never do it—to never beat yourself up about not having done it, to never spend another moment worrying about it. If you commit to it, please take that very seriously. You are making a promise to yourself, and you're going to have to live with yourself for a good long time, so please treat yourself with *at least* the respect you show other people and be good to your word.

> If you make a commitment to yourself, keep it.

If you decide you are not ever going to do an item—congratulations! You have just completed an undone. Cross it off your list!

If you are having trouble deciding, and you're simply not willing to make a decision right now (don't say "can't" make a decision!), then that decision itself becomes a new undone. You can either write "—decision" after the original item, or add a new item at the bottom of the list. But it's not going to go away.

For the items you are committed to do, write "—committed" after each item. You are not done with this step until every item on your list is either crossed out or has "—committed" written after it. Commit to the "decision" ones, too, if you have any of those. Please do this now. If you have a good (or flimsy) reason why not, add that to your "Excuses" list—and do it anyway!

STEP 3: DO IT!

You now have a list of things you are committed to do. How do you feel? For me, "sober" is the best word to describe how I felt the first time I did this process. When I realized I was actually going to do the things I had told myself I would, I suddenly started to put a lot more thought into what I promised myself. No more "I'll pay the bills tomorrow" unless I really meant it! No more "I'll get up at 6 a.m.," followed by an hour and a half of snooze alarms. No more "I'll start my diet tomorrow morning" or "I'll go to Aerobics on Wednesday." (Notice how a lot of these half-hearted non-commitments are the result of my avoiding something I don't feel like doing right now. Don't compound an avoider by creating another undone or setting yourself up to break a commitment!)

So, sober, excited, or whatever—it's time to start thinking about actually doing these undones. Remember, these are things you *want to* do, either on their own merits or to prevent the negative consequences of not doing them. So enjoy the process.

If there are any undones you are willing to handle right now, go for it! You can cross each one off your list as it's handled. If you can't do any right now because you don't have a bookmark, add "I don't have a bookmark" to your list of excuses and do them anyway. When you come back, turn to page 87.

CONTINUE READING HERE

OK. So you've done all the undones you're willing to do right now, and we'll have to schedule the rest. (If that sounds scary, feel free to handle some more right now.) Get out your date book and open it up to today. If you have some time to do this scheduling thing right now, great—otherwise, find some free time and write in "Schedule Undones" and I'll see you then. If you're ready, here we go!

Go back to the top of the list. For every item on the list, decide when you are going to do it, block out the time in your calendar, and write it in. If it's a BIG undone, like "get Ph.D." or "improve relationship with mother," schedule out at least the first step. Some people like to work forwards, and some like to work backwards: for instance, if your undone is "build house," you could work forwards, breaking off a manageable first step such as "go to drafting supply store and purchase architectural drawing tools" or even "apply to architecture school." Or you could work backwards with a goal of having the house built in three years, blocking out a day three years from now for "throw housewarming party," and filling in all the things you'll need to do between now and then to get it completed. Or you could combine the two, blocking out next Saturday afternoon for "develop house-building schedule."

If an undone seems too big or too scary, just do one small step. If that step is too hard, do a smaller step. If even the smallest step is too hard—add "It's too hard" to your list of excuses, then schedule in an hour to brainstorm by yourself or with a friend about possible next steps.

> It's always possible to break down any undone, no matter how big, to a manageable next step.

When you have scheduled a time to do each undone, put a check mark next to it. Don't cross it off yet—save that pleasure for when you actually complete it. If you've scheduled just a next step for some of them, rather than the whole thing, be honest with yourself: are you really making progress, or are you just putting it off? Even the smallest step, such as the brainstorming session, is real progress—just don't cheat yourself. You know the difference.

If you're resisting scheduling things because you're not 100% sure you can make the schedule—add "I'm not 100% sure I can make the schedule" to your list of excuses, and see the chapter on perfectionism. As long as you honestly intend to do the things as scheduled, it's fine to be flexible and reschedule (preferably for an earlier, not later, time). It may turn out that the housewarming party fell on the same day as your Ph.D. graduation ceremony—no problem to move the party up a week. Just be honest and don't cheat yourself. And do it!

If you're stuck trying to come up with a next step,
make your next step be a brainstorming session.

10

◆

Perfectionism

Man errs as long as he strives.
—Johann Wolfgang von Goethe

I know I had heard the saying "nobody's perfect" when I was growing up; I just think somehow I missed the fact that it applied to me, too. I don't think it was vanity or ego that contributed most to my perfectionism; I was just deathly afraid of being caught doing something wrong. Ironically, it was just that fear that got me into the most trouble.

PERFECTION AND AGREEMENTS

A friend recently told me, with a mixture of excitement and trepidation, that he had finally figured out the value of keeping agreements with himself.

He had always been meticulous about keeping his word with me and with other people he considered important in his life, and often structured his time so that nothing short of a major disaster could interfere with his keeping appointments he had made with me, even if they were appointments that I considered casual social engagements that could be rescheduled without much problem.

He made up for his super-earnestness in keeping agreements with "important" people by the way he viewed agreements with himself or with "unimportant" people such as salespersons: he would break those agreements without thinking twice. This was necessary so that he could have the flexibility necessary to keep those "important" agreements.

When he realized breaking the agreements with himself was damaging his self-acceptance and therefore hindering the progress he wanted to make toward improving his quality of life—when he *got* that, it was only a few seconds before he reacted in alarm:

"If that's true, then I'm never going to make another agreement with myself—or anyone!"

Ignoring the fact that he had just made another agreement with himself by saying he was never going to make one, his conclusion underscored one of the key self-sabotaging beliefs of the perfectionist: that nothing less than perfect is acceptable.

The point of keeping agreements is to build trust in ourselves so when we commit to something important to us we have a decent chance of succeeding. Now, one failure is not going to destroy our self-trust any more than forgetting one lunch date is going to destroy a relationship. But looking at those failures can teach us a lot about what's really going on.

LEARNING FROM FAILURE

I'm grumbling as I type this, just because I was such a perfectionist as I was growing up that I hated hearing that I should "learn from my mistakes." All I heard was that I was bad for making mistakes, and if I was good, I'd learn not to make any more of them!

That's not what I mean. But for me, it took a while to unwind my self-critical, perfectionist tendency to the point where I was willing to *really* learn from my mistakes and failures. So what do I think it *is* appropriate to learn from failure? First off, it's *not* how to never fail in the future.

> People who never fail are people who never take risks. Failure means you had the courage to try something beyond what was safe. If you want to have a great life, you'll be risking, and failing, more than people who are just surviving.

If you fail, take a look at what you're allowing to be more important that what you failed at. It could either be something that is truly more important—in which case there's nothing wrong; you just made a choice—or it could be something that isn't as important to you: a distraction, avoider, unconscious pattern, or whatever.

When you are weighing whether something else was truly more important than doing what you committed to, remember: keeping your agreements with yourself has its own value over and above the result of making the goal. Most people pay more attention to keeping their agreements with other people than they do to keeping agreements with themselves. But I'm *not* saying that agreements with other people are unimportant; in fact:

> Any agreement with someone else, if you're sincere about it, is also an agreement with yourself. Breaking it hurts you.

When you do fail at keeping an agreement or at something else, you have an opportunity to increase your self-acceptance. Cut yourself some slack! Don't whip yourself because you failed—that will just lower your self-acceptance and make it more difficult to succeed in the future. Instead, congratulate yourself for risking. Re-focus on what's most important to you; notice any patterns of avoiding what's important; and recommit to your goal.

INTENTION VERSUS RESULTS

The biggest trap about perfectionism is that it distracts us from *actually doing* what's most important. If we spend as much of our time and energy as possible doing what's most important to us, we will have the best results possible. Maybe not perfect results, but the best results possible. Time spent worrying doesn't help.

If you have perfectionist tendencies, and you find yourself worrying about results, make that a signal to re-focus on your intentions. What is most important to you?

GUILT

The main icky feeling accompanying perfectionism is guilt. I am not a fan of guilt, although there are some popular religions that make it practically a cornerstone. Since this book is about enjoying life, though, I'm going to talk about how to get rid of it. If you enjoy guilt, you can skip this part.

Part of the stress I built up when I was going through the most difficult period of my life was in the form of loads and loads of guilt hanging over my head. The more guilt I had, the more stressed I got. The more stressed I got, the more things I did that I felt guilty for. I had no idea how to get out of that cycle short of turning tail and running away, which I eventually did.

Before you call the FBI to come investigate these things I felt guilty about, let me give you two examples:

- Sometimes I goofed off during working hours.
- There were some parts of my job that I felt unqualified for.

Ooh, it still tugs at my gut just to write that. I goof off a lot less now that it's out in the open, but years ago I had a belief, probably acquired from watching "Leave It to Beaver," that good people (Ward Cleaver) focused effectively on their highest-priority work all day long and never got distracted, took breaks, or indulged themselves (Fred Rutherford). If I goofed off, I wasn't a good person.

So now I had a dilemma: I wanted to be a good person, but I was doing all these things I believed a good person wouldn't do.

> Feeling guilty is a signal that our image of ourselves does not match who we really are.

The truth was, I *was* goofing off, there *were* parts of my job I didn't know how to do, and I wasn't doing anything about it! Not only did I have the guilt, but I stayed stuck right in my dilemma.

I think people have a myth that guilt motivates them to change, and I think it's one of the most bogus myths we have. My mother is a wonderful human being, but she has felt guilty about not writing letters to people for more than 60 years, and she still hasn't changed. Guilt gives people the illusion they're doing something about the problem, but leaves them stuck right where they are. Besides, it feels awful.

So, if guilt is a red flag signaling us we have an inaccurate image of ourselves, what can we do about it? Two things: change our image of ourselves, or change our behavior.

If you have any perfectionist tendencies at all, I recommend starting by changing your image of yourself, just to cut yourself some slack. Good people do have flaws—even good diamonds do. Even the Sun has sunspots. I've made some big, big mistakes in my life, and I'm doing just fine. It won't hurt, only help, to live in the reality of who you are right now. Accept yourself first, then change if you still want to.

If part of your image is that you *always* do something or you *never* do something, please realize: you're not helping yourself or anyone by lying to yourself. Pretending you're perfect when you're not makes it *harder* to achieve excellence. Mom, you don't tend to write letters. Richard, there are parts of your job you don't know how to do. It's puzzling, but the most effective way to change yourself is first to change your self-image in the other direction—to match the current reality. After that, it's easier to change.

Or—dare I suggest?—once you get your self-image to match reality, and give up the futile pursuit of perfection, you may be surprised to find you're suddenly OK with the way you are.

11

◆

Power

There are people who have money and people who are rich.

—Coco Chanel

Why is it some people seem to have lots of power, and some people don't? I'm not talking about world leaders or elected officials; that's a different kind of power. I'm talking about the bossy coworker who always seems to get his or her way, the relative whom the family always seems to have to plan around, or the sales clerk who gets away with being rude and self-centered while the rest of us are more sensitive and polite. Who gives them that power?

You do.

This chapter is about how to keep your power, rather than give it away.

THE VICTIM MINDSET

When I was a kid, one of the most effective ways of dealing with an injustice, such as my brother taking one of my toys, was to kick and scream and complain it was "not fair"! If I protested loud enough and long enough, my parents would right the wrong, punish the transgressor, and perhaps compensate me in some way for the injustice. (I was particularly partial to cake and ice cream.)

Being a kid, I had extremely limited power to right any wrongs myself, especially if the wrongdoers were bigger or outnumbered me. Trying to stand up for myself against such villains as Eighth-Graders or Big Dogs was ineffective at best, and in some cases could result in severe bodily harm.

Some kids have parents who are so sensitive to the cries of "not fair" and so quick to compensate any perceived injustice—such as the lack of designer jeans, a private telephone line, a Ferrari—that these kids learn proclaiming themselves a victim is an extremely effective strategy for getting what they want. These kids are sometimes known as "spoiled brats."

The rest of us, the unspoiled, the common kid, the pure of heart, simply learn that justice sometimes, if not always, prevails. The victim gets compensated, the guilty one is punished, and the wrong is righted. That's what I learned as a kid.

> The trouble starts when we bring that "victim" mentality we learned as children into our lives as adults, and fail to realize that we now have other options for dealing with injustice.

For the big, terrible injustices we occasionally encounter as adults, we of course have the court system available to us. Judging from the ever-increasing amount of litigation that is going on in this country, I don't need to spend too much space discussing that option. That is the grown-up version of crying "not fair" to our parents.

For life's minor injustices, though, playing that "victim" role, *even though it may be completely justified,* is a poor strategy for actually getting anything accomplished that would improve our quality of life.

If we had fairy godparents flying above us who would hear our cries of "not fair!" and wave their wands to correct the situation, things might be different. But we don't. The only thing likely to happen is our friends will get tired of listening to us complain. What *won't* happen is anything to improve the situation: all that energy we spend looking backwards at the "victim" incident is energy we *don't* spend on what is most important to us.

Complaining things are "not fair"
works best if you have a fairy godparent.

I'm not saying you don't deserve to be upset, feel pain, be sad, or grieve when something unfair happens to you. But for adults, the "prove it's not fair" and "I'm a victim" attitudes are *ineffective* at setting things right or improving our lives. The predominant feeling that goes along with the victim attitude is self-pity: we replay the hurt over and over, as if we could somehow right the wrong by proving it should never have happened.

> We get to choose our attitudes. If you feel self-pity, or notice yourself with a victim attitude, let it serve as a signal to re-focus on what's most important to you. And that's *not* proving it's "not fair."

Now the good news: as adults, we have a lot more power and options available to us than we did as kids. So if we adopt an attitude that makes use of all that power and all the choices we have the power to make as adults, we will be much more effective at getting what we want out of life.

ACCOUNTABILITY

President Truman made famous the saying on a sign he had on his desk in the Oval Office: "The buck stops here." He knew the President of the United States had more power than probably anyone else in the world, and his refusal to pass the buck on any problem or issue that came his way reflected his willingness to use that power to actually get things done. Other Presidents have blamed Congress, the economy, past Presidents, or anything they could think of to avoid taking responsibility for problems. Truman knew blame doesn't solve problems.

If you want to have the greatest life possible, let the buck stop with you. Every time you pass the buck, by assigning blame, saying it's not fair, saying it shouldn't have happened (and between you and me—I know it shouldn't have, not to a nice person like *you*)—every time you say it's someone else's fault, it's not your problem—you give away *the power you already have* to improve the situation.

Accountability is an attitude you can choose, just like the ineffective victim attitude. If you choose to be accountable, you're simply saying "the buck stops here." You are owning the situation, regardless of whose fault it was. You aren't wasting energy trying to assign fault or blame, even to yourself!

> When you are accountable, you are saying, "I made some choices, and from those choices came my results."

The victim attitude is more like "stuff happened to me that I didn't deserve and it's not fair." Notice the two are not mutually exclusive! If you want to spend time and energy proving you *didn't deserve* to have that meteorite crash through your roof and destroy your fish tank, fine—I won't argue with you. I could point out you chose to live in that house, buy a fish tank, and put it right in that spot, but what would be the use?

It's not a question of which point of view is "true," victim or accountability—like all those old sayings that contradict each other, they're just different ways of looking at the same thing. The difference is, choosing the victim attitude tends to keep us frustrated and stuck, while choosing the accountable attitude tends to launch us toward action and solution.

I think most people realize choosing accountability makes sense for areas of their life where they clearly see they have lots of choices and a large amount of control. For instance, even before I had heard the term "accountability," I was always accountable for the computer programs I wrote. It was just obvious to me that the computer was completely controlled by the program I wrote, so if anything went wrong, it had to be some problem with the instructions I gave the computer. I never wasted any time or energy trying to assign blame, or finding fault—I just went over the program I had written and looked for the problem. Being accountable helped me focus my resources on what was most important to me.

On the other hand, the first time I heard someone talk about accountability, I said to myself, "Come on—what about something like a traffic jam? How could I be accountable for that? I'm stuck behind it!" It didn't make sense to me. I knew I often had a terrible time driving through traffic jams—it seemed like such a waste to me—but I didn't see how I could be accountable.

Well, I soon had a chance to find out. A few days later, I found myself caught in a full-blown backup taking the bridge home over Lake Washington. Having just taken a seminar on accountability, I noticed I was choosing a victim attitude, fuming to myself about how unlucky I was to get caught in this thing, how the whole city was going to pot, and what were all these other turkeys doing on the road, etc. "Hmm," I thought. "Let's experiment with this 'accountability' stuff."

So I consciously thought, "OK, this traffic jam is the result of choices I made. Huh? How does that work?" And then it hit me: "Oh! *Sitting* in this traffic jam is the result of choices I made!" It was indeed. At once, as a result of my choosing the position of accountability, two things happened.

First, I immediately felt better. All the unpleasant feelings of unfairness, powerlessness, frustration, and self-pity quickly faded, replaced by a feeling that I was much more powerful and in control.

Second, I became conscious of some alternative choices I could have made that would have kept me out of the traffic. I could have taken the other bridge over Lake Washington, which is usually clear but adds about 10 miles to the trip. I could have done some shopping in the city, waiting until after rush hour to drive home. I could have scheduled my appointment downtown for midday rather than late afternoon.

Choosing accountability as a point of view gives you a double benefit: you tend to feel powerful rather than frustrated or helpless, and you automatically focus your resources on solving problems and moving ahead with what's most important to you. You enjoy life more, and you're more effective at the same time. What a deal!

> It's not a question of having to *prove* you are account-able for things. Accountability is just a point of view. It is neither more nor less "true" than the victim point of view. It just works a whole lot better.

100% ACCOUNTABILITY

Because choosing accountability works so well as a way to maximize the power you have over your life, I'm going to ask you to choose to be 100% accountable. That means you are willing to be accountable for *everything* that has happened or will happen to you in your life, good or bad.

Now don't go off proving you couldn't possibly be accountable for this or that—remember, I'm not saying you're *to blame* for things; I'm just saying it's to your advantage to choose to look at things through the eyes of accountability, *because it's the most effective attitude to take.*

> 100% accountability maximizes the power you have over your own life. It's taking the position, "From all of my choices come all of my results."

If you're like me, you're looking for the hole in this theory, or some counterexample to contradict it. That's not necessary; remember, I'm not saying it's *true!* Just as the same glass can be half-empty or half-full, you can look at any event or situation in your life as something that was *done to you,* or as *resulting from your choices.*

Granted, there's not too much value in trying to figure out what choices you could have made differently in the case of the meteorite smashing your fish tank. But there's no harm in being accountable for that, too. For some things, you made the best choices you could, you got a crummy result, and leave it at that. The real value comes from the power you get when the accountable point of view spotlights important choices that the victim point of view wouldn't illuminate.

LET'S BE REALISTIC

I know some wonderful, intelligent, sensible people who were initially unwilling to look at things from the point of view of 100% accountability. They would say things like, "You're telling me if I'm standing on a pier admiring the sunset, and a man comes up from behind me and pushes me into the water, that I *chose* that? That's just not realistic!"

But that's not what I mean by accountability.

> Being accountable does not mean you *wanted* a particular result. It means seeing that the result stems from choices *you* have made. They may have been the best possible choices available, or they may not.

Just as betting on the favorite in a horse race does not guarantee success, neither does making the best possible choices guarantee the best possible results. If a man pushes me off a pier, he has done a bad thing and deserves to be punished. My being accountable doesn't change that—I'm *accountable*, not *guilty*. But even so, there are choices I could make differently next time to keep it from happening.

I could choose to turn my head and look behind me every few seconds. I could choose to bring a friend or a dog with me next time. I could choose to hire a bodyguard. If it happens more than once, I'm going to start examining my choices more closely—do I have a "push me" sign taped to my back? And if I am absolutely unwilling to risk the small possibility of being pushed off a pier, I'll choose to stay off piers!

Now, *should I have to* do any of these things? Is it *fair*? Is it *my fault*? These are all questions that come from the victim attitude and do nothing to increase the quality of my life. No matter how airtight a case I make that what happened *shouldn't* have happened and *wasn't my fault,* it won't help me have a great life.

The value in choosing to be 100% accountable does not come in unusual situations such as the pier-pushing or the meteorite. It comes in everyday life, in places where the tendency is to get stuck in the "not fair" syndrome—in the little or big things that bug you on the job or in your relationships. Choosing accountability instead of the victim point of view gives *you* your power back and focuses your resources on what's most important to you.

A LEAP OF FAITH

It's possible this is the first time you've thought of an attitude as something you *consciously choose,* rather than just something you have. It may seem uncomfortable or phony to look at things through accountable eyes rather than the victim outlook your unconscious has selected for you. You may see intellectually how 100% accountability is a good idea, but right now you just don't have a feel for how it would work or how you would do it. If that's the case, you might try taking a leap of faith and just doing it to see what happens.

Faith means believing without proof. When it comes to making a conscious choice to switch attitudes or points of view, it's often difficult to understand what the value of doing so would be—or even to believe it's possible—before you actually do it. I know so many people who have found 100% accountability to be an effective, empowering point of view that I can recommend without hesitation that you at least try it out on faith. Especially if you already have an accountable attitude in some areas of your life, see what happens when you give yourself that power in your whole life.

Make a commitment that, for the next seven days, you will look at your life with the attitude of 100% accountability. Every time you feel self-pity, or you notice yourself looking at something with the victim attitude, consciously switch to an accountable point of view. Try it for a week, and see what happens. Take a leap of faith!

12

◆

Breaking Patterns

Snakes! Why does it always have to be snakes?
—Indiana Jones,
"Raiders of the Lost Ark"

Most of the choices we make every day, we make unconsciously. There's nothing wrong with that, of course; the more choices we delegate to our unconscious, the more energy we leave for our conscious mind to do what it does best: reason, plan, be creative, solve problems, and so on. We often call an unconscious choice we make after something happens a *reaction* to that event. I'll use the word *response* for the conscious equivalent of that: a thoughtful, reasoned choice—thinking before acting, if you will.

Our unconscious minds get filled with all kinds of little programmed reactions to various events. One way they get there is if we repeat the same response to something many times; pretty soon, it becomes unconscious, or second nature. (I guess "first nature" would be the genetic reflex reactions we are born with, such as contracting our pupils in reaction to bright light, or kicking in response to a doctor's tapping our knee.) Just as an actor memorizes lines to a play, our unconscious memorizes the way we act and feel in response to various situations. All these patterns we learn hang out in our unconscious, ready to be triggered by whatever circumstances activate them.

Driving a car is one example of a routine that starts as a whole series of conscious responses and becomes more a set of unconscious reactions as we gain experience. When I started to drive, I remember my father grimacing and clutching the armrests as I bucked the car back and forth, trying to figure out exactly how to engage and release the clutch in response to the sound and feel of the engine.

If you asked me today if I used the clutch last time I drove my car, the best answer I would give is that, logically, since I got the car from there to here and I had to step on the clutch to do that, I must have! But it was far from conscious. Automobile accidents are often the result of our not reacting quickly to an unusual situation that comes up—since we have not practiced it, we don't have it in our repertoire of reactions. There are special driving schools to practice responding to unusual road hazards so you develop the reactions necessary to handle them if they ever come up.

Smoking cigarettes is another pattern that gets ingrained through conscious repetition. Many smokers will tell you that smoking their first few cigarettes felt unnatural and uncomfortable, if not painful! And yet, through many repetitions, that habit becomes ingrained—impressed into a set of unconscious reactions. Why do many people have difficulty quitting smoking, even after dealing with the physical addiction to nicotine? Because their un-conscious minds are mined, so to speak, with trigger after trigger as-sociating various situations with the act of lighting up a cigarette (and the associated feelings). There's the coffee-break cigarette, the after-dinner cigarette, the cigarette after—well, you get the picture. Any successful program to support people to quit smoking has to deal with the presence of all this unconscious baggage reinforcing the habit.

So we can create patterns of unconscious reactions—useful, harmful, mixed, or indifferent—through many repetitions of a conscious response. But we can also develop these unconscious re-actions without involving our conscious mind at all. For instance, through my experiences growing up in the public schools, where I probably received no more than the average amount of teasing and harassment from the other students, I developed a pattern of distrust for people who wanted something from me.

Unconscious patterns of behavior learned long ago can still be around today, causing problems without us even being aware of them.

Now this was completely reasonable, because I remember several incidents where I good-naturedly went along with what the other kid wanted, only to be surprised by a punch in the gut or humiliated by some name-calling. I don't remember ever making a conscious choice not to trust people, but my unconscious mind sure set up that pattern, which worked fine through junior high school, then started getting in my way, especially when I wanted to have relationships with women.

Remember, this was all completely unconscious! Unlike smoking or overeating, where it's at least easy to identify the pattern, I didn't even know I had a pattern of distrusting people that was getting in my way. It was just me, doing my life, day by day. I had no idea there was this unconscious pattern going on! I didn't figure it out until I got feedback from other people in an experiential workshop designed to help people become conscious of this type of thing.

Now suppose I have some kind of "bad habit" or pattern in my life, something I keep doing over and over, even though when I consciously think about it, I say to myself, "Why do I do that? I don't like that!" It could be a physical thing such as smoking or overeating, or a more general pattern such as procrastination or a difficulty saying "no," or even a subtle, hidden pattern such as my tendency to distrust people. How do I get rid of it? Why do these things have power over me?

It's not as simple as saying, "OK, unconscious: please stop that pattern." It's much easier to get these patterns or reactions started up than to shut them down. Once they get started, they operate independently.

I know of two approaches to the problem of dealing with destructive unconscious reactions. For either approach you need a very clear idea about what is most important to you in life. Because if you aren't clear about that, then not only is there very little incentive for you to change, but it's not clear which patterns are destructive, constructive, or indifferent! There's a tendency to waffle back and forth to the point of frustration, then throw up your hands and forget the problem until it comes up next time. If you don't feel clear about what is most important to you in life, I highly recommend you do what it takes to figure it out. I'll have lots more to say about that later.

R E S P O N D   V E R S U S   R E A C T

The first approach to breaking destructive patterns involves this notion of responding rather than reacting to situations. If you are very clear about what is most important to you, and you have identified a pattern in your life that you consider destructive, you can intervene consciously every time the issue comes up and make a conscious response rather than an unconscious reaction. This only works well if you are clear about something more important than just continuing the pattern, and if you are strongly committed to it!

As an example, my father smoked cigarettes for more than 20 years, from the time he was in the Navy until my brother and I were in grade school. One day, he had severe chest pains and was rushed to the hospital, where the doctors decided the chest pains were a "false alarm" rather than a heart attack. Although the diagnosis brought everyone relief, the episode was enough to persuade my father to quit smoking cigarettes. Displaying uncommon wisdom about his own nature, Dad decided the best way to guarantee he would quit smoking was to make a solemn promise to my brother and me that he would never smoke another cigarette. I remember the occasion vividly, since it seemed so momentous and serious.

My father understood that to break the pattern he needed to be very clear about something that was more important to him than the pleasure, relaxation, comfort, and whatever else smoking brought him. For him, that was the importance of keeping his word to his children. And to my knowledge, he never smoked another cigarette.

So for the respond-versus-react method to work in breaking patterns, here are the steps:

1.   Be clear about something that is more important to you than continuing the pattern.
2.   Commit to it.
3.   As you become aware of situations where you would tend to *react* as part of the unconscious pattern, stop, notice your tendency, and instead make a conscious *response* in line with your commitment.

If you're saying this is simplistic, you've tried this and it's harder than that—take another look. Did you skip over the first two steps? This is not an exercise in will power. The trouble with depending on will power—and I've used will power "successfully" (short term) many times—is you've only got one will. Not only do we tend to bounce back to the old pattern as soon as we let up and focus our will power on something else, but it's often an unpleasant, grueling, ulcer-inducing experience to drag ourselves through life against all our unconscious tendencies solely through the use of will power. I'm not talking about will power.

If you take the first two steps seriously—make it a priority to get crystal clear about what is most important to you in your life, and then commit to it, you will find the third step—actually following through on your commitment—to be not only possible, but an empowering, self-honoring experience: just the opposite of forcing yourself through will power and self-criticism. Know what's most important to you. What else is there to do?

THE SUBSTITUTION METHOD

The second approach involves substitution. One treatment for people addicted to the drug heroin is to substitute a less addictive drug, methadone, to fill the needs of the addict. They then lower the dosage of the substitute gradually, slowly eliminating the body's physical need for the drug. (By my thinking, unless a constructive substitute shows up to fill whatever *mental* need the drug was filling, this treatment is not likely to succeed long term.)

The substitution approach works on the theory that many of the patterns we have that we don't particularly find constructive are actually giving us some kind of short-term gain. The long-term cost is usually apparent, but often the short-term gain fueling the pattern is not so obvious. On a physical level, this is the theory behind the nicotine-chewing-gum method of quitting smoking. The nicotine and chewing sensation are supposed to replace the body's need for smoking a cigarette with a less harmful substitute.

You can apply this theory to one of your habits or patterns that you want to change. First, figure out what the short-term gain to you is in the habit. For smoking, it could be relaxation, a sense of independence, a feeling of fitting in or belonging if your friends smoke, or something else.

Once you have identified the short-term gain or gains in the pattern you don't like, the next step is to get creative and come up with some other ways to satisfy that need. Just as finding another way to fill the physical cravings assists the drug addict or smoker to quit, when you find new ways to achieve the mental gains that were being filled by the undesirable pattern, you will find it much easier to break the pattern.

Once again, though, the first step is to get clear on exactly what these experiences are that you are craving, the needs that are being filled short-term by these patterns that you consciously say you don't want. Because unconsciously, you're shouting back, "Yes I do! _____ is very important to me!" Fill in the blank with the short-term gain you are getting through the otherwise destructive behavior. There's something there, otherwise you wouldn't keep doing it. And when you are clear about what those cravings are, you can go to the next step: create new patterns in your life that fill those cravings in a constructive, not destructive, way.

To sum up, here are the steps involved in the substitution approach to breaking destructive patterns:

1. Get clear about what need or craving is being filled by the pattern. There must be some short-term gain, or you wouldn't keep doing it.
2. Get creative about some new ways to fill that craving—ways that are constructive, rather than destructive to your life overall.
3. As the cravings are filled in other ways, it becomes easier to break the pattern by conscious choice.

THE BACKSTAGE METHOD

I'm going to throw in one more thing to complete this chapter on breaking patterns. It's fun, and it actually worked for me once, in spite of my bias toward rational thought and my general skepticism of anything weird. One theory on the function of dreaming is that we resolve issues or work out problems through dreams, without conscious, rational thought. I remember times when I have been stumped for an answer to a difficult computer-programming problem—and computer programming is about as logical and rational as you can get—and the next morning, having slept on it, found the answer had popped into my head. This variation on the substitution method involves throwing the whole mess to your unconscious and trusting that part of yourself to come up with a solution "backstage," without conscious involvement.

You can try this next exercise with a friend, reading to each other, or you can re-read it enough times to become familiar with it and do it yourself. The important thing is that you be relaxed, comfortable, and have faith in the power of your unconscious to handle this.

Relax, breathe comfortably, and direct your thoughts to the part of your unconscious mind that is in charge of giving you what you want. Relax, and talk, for now, with the part of your unconscious that works behind the scenes, making sure you are safe and happy.

Ask your unconscious, "Hello, unconscious. Would you be willing to work together to change one of our patterns that doesn't seem to be working well for us?" Wait until you have a sense that your unconscious is there and ready to help.

Now bring to mind one of your patterns that you consider less than constructive. Ask your unconscious to become aware of this pattern. Now ask your unconscious, "In what way are you using this pattern to benefit me? What is the gain for me in this pattern?" If you do get an answer from your unconscious, make a mental note of it. If nothing comes to mind, that's OK.

Now direct your thoughts to the creative part of your unconscious, the part of you that comes up with new ideas, plans, and strategies. Tell your creative part, "I'd like you to come up with at least three new constructive ways to get

"Hello, unconscious? Have this on my desk by 9 a.m., please."

me the same benefit. Please create at least three new ways
to give me the same gain, ways that are supportive of
everything else that is important to me." Trust your
unconscious to do this on its own, without becoming aware
of the three new strategies. Wait until you have a sense
that the process is complete.

Now tell your whole unconscious, "Please use these new
ways, which are supportive and constructive, to get me
that benefit. I appreciate your support of me, and I trust
and respect the way that you assist me. Thanks, and we'll
talk more later!"

When you're ready, take a deep breath, and the process is
complete.

If something did pop into your head when you asked what the
benefit was to the destructive pattern, remember it! It could be one
of the core experiences that are important to you, and it's good to
know what those are! If nothing came to mind, or if it was something negative, don't worry. There's a lot of emotionally charged
baggage associated with these destructive patterns, and it may take
peeling away many layers to get down to the core. Keep going!

13

♦

Self-Fulfilling Prophecy

Don't be superstitious—it's bad luck!

> —*Finian,*
> *"Finian's Rainbow"*

One of my favorite childhood stories was "The Little Engine That Could," the story of the railroad engine who made it up a steep hill powered by his belief that "I can." I remember being impressed by the idea that the engine, or I, had the power to make important things happen just by thinking. It seemed like magic!

Of course, the truth is the engine had the *ability* to get up that hill all along, but the strong belief "I can" helped focus that ability to get the job done. This is the whole theory behind positive thinking, creative visualization, affirmations, and the idea of *self-fulfilling prophecy.* The very act of believing that something is possible or will happen helps to increase the chances of success. Conversely, believing something is difficult or unlikely can sabotage success. As Henry Ford said, whether you think you can or you can't—you're right!

Remember, you get to choose your beliefs. Why would you choose beliefs that sabotage you, even if you think they are true? So what if it's true right now?

> If you *utterly refuse* to believe that you *can't, are unable, are limited,* or *don't deserve,* you will *automatically* make faster progress toward what is most important to you.

POSITIVE THINKING AND THE "PSYCH"

I highly recommend positive thinking in any situation where you're committed to a goal. What I mean by that is, believe you will succeed, and don't fill your head with thoughts about how you might fail. Of course you might! But you're more likely to succeed if you believe you will succeed.

When his team is behind at half-time of a football game, does the coach sit down with the players and say, "Listen, fellas—we're down by a touchdown. Statistically speaking, we have only a 23% chance of coming from behind and winning the game"? No! He says, "Come on, men! We're better than this team, and every one of you knows it! And we're going to win! We're going to come out fighting, hit 'em left, right, left, right! Go! Go! Go!" This is known as "psyching up"—creating a positive self-fulfilling prophecy. The team is more likely to win, and if they lose, they probably enjoyed the second half all the more for trying harder.

The opposite of this is known as "psyching out"—creating a negative self-fulfilling prophecy in your opponent, as when a tennis player shows off a new, $900 racquet and mentions that he felt like he had to buy it since he was just named number-one seed at the club. His hope is that you will buy into his manipulative act and create a belief that he is better than you, which will sabotage your chances of winning.

My mother took her job of raising my brother and me very seriously. She researched the subject thoroughly, in the process collecting so many books on child-rearing and relationships that we spent one weekend building shelves in the garage for the overflow. I discussed the subject with her some years ago, and she said the most important thing she felt she did was to help us believe in our own ability. She did it not only by constantly telling us how wonderful we were and that we could do anything we set our mind to, but also by making sure that opportunities were available to us that fit our interests.

Believing in your own success or failure can
help make it happen—in life and other games.

For example, I must have studied seven different musical instruments as a child, and not once did she tell me that I "couldn't" take up a new one—she just got them on the rent-to-own plan and returned them when I lost interest. I remember her surprise when I finally settled on the clarinet, and we had rented it enough months that we owned it. I eventually went on to become a fine Third Clarinet player in the Harvard Band.

Through the combination of telling us we had ability and actually creating opportunities for us that validated that belief, she did raise us with a strong sense of "I can," which has served me well all my life.

AFFIRMATIONS

An affirmation is a positive statement, in the present tense, about something you want to be true, although you might have some doubt about it. For example:

- I am making progress toward having a fantastic life.
- I have good taste.
- I trust my own judgment.
- I can do anything I set my mind to.

People who use affirmations typically say them aloud one or more times a day. The idea is to reinforce your sense of ability, and to strengthen points of view that help keep you on track to what is most important to you (like getting over the hill, for The Little Engine That Could). These statements should be positive, not negative (i.e., don't use "I am not a complete loser"), and they should be things you really do believe, even if you have doubts or conflicting beliefs.

Don't lie to yourself! The point here is to increase, not decrease, self-acceptance. If you tell yourself lies in the form of affirmations that are not true, how are you supposed to trust yourself? I would recommend limiting your use of affirmations to beliefs that you already accept at a gut level, but you question or doubt on some other level, or for psyching yourself up for the best possible result of your endeavor, a result that is possible even if not guaranteed or even likely.

> When you're using positive thinking or affirmations, it's still important to be honest with yourself. There's a big difference between refusing to hold self-sabotaging beliefs and telling yourself lies in the hopes that they will come true.

CREATIVE VISUALIZATION

Creating a mental image of a desired result is a great way to focus and motivate yourself. Often, when I feel reluctant to start writing or programming (usually at one of the hard parts like the beginning of a new chapter or software module), I'll visualize myself sitting at a table in my favorite bookstore, signing autographs for a crowd of people who are waving copies of my book above their heads and jostling for position. Or I'll visualize myself showing off how the program I'm writing works to a crowd of excited coworkers who are patting me on the back and telling me what a great job I did. (This is called "creative" visualization—get creative!)

The mental image can contain pictures, sounds, feelings, emotions—whatever you can imagine. In that way, it's an efficient way of packaging lots of mini-affirmations into one visualization.

On the flip side, do you ever find yourself imagining *negative* results? Get those self-sabotaging images out of your head, because the undesirable images can create just as much of a self-fulfilling prophecy as the desirable ones. If you like, when a negative image pops into your head, take a mental sledge hammer and smash it to pieces! Then replace it with an image of the best possible result of your endeavor.

You Still Have To Work

Remember—the tools I'm talking about in this book are designed to *help you* succeed in whatever your purpose is. Don't use them *instead of* actually spending your time, money, and energy on what is most important to you.

I don't know how many times I've heard people who have been through personal-growth workshops start to use the tools and jargon they've learned to make new, clever excuses, justifications, and avoiders. So if you catch yourself saying or thinking things like

- I know I haven't spent too much time looking for a new job, but I am visualizing success!
- I didn't call Fred and resolve that issue, so I guess it wasn't truly important to me.
- I'm not going to exercise today after all, because I want to keep my agreement not to be so hard on myself.

add them to your list of excuses, and *do it anyway!*

Visualizing success doesn't do much for you if you're not willing to spend your time, money, and energy on it. Lying to yourself about what's really important to you to justify past results doesn't work either. And breaking an agreement is breaking an agreement, no matter how good your excuse is. Be honest.

14

◆

Communication and Feedback

Oh, would some power the giftie gie us
To see ourselves as others see us.
It would from many a blunder free us
And foolish notion.

—Robert Burns

So far, I've had a lot of chapters about you, but I haven't written much about the other people in your life. You may find it useful in your quest to have a great life, however, to include other people from time to time. And in fact, other people can often be eager to help you, and be of great aid to you in increasing your understanding and acceptance of yourself. So I'm devoting this chapter not specifically to communicating within Big, Meaningful Relationships, but rather to communicating with people in general.

I'm going to start with this, since this important point seems to be lost on many people:

> Communication involves two parts:
> talking and listening.

Assuming you're not already a perfect communicator: if you're a fabulous talker, a noted raconteur, your growth potential may be in the area of listening. If you're a great listener, someone to whom people feel *so* comfortable coming for a sympathetic ear, your opportunity may be in sharpening your talking skills. The rest of you — well, read both parts.

LISTENING

As much as I hate jargon, I don't know a better word to communicate the idea I want to get across than *feedback*. Feedback is a term swiped from the world of electronics. When some circuit is designed to have an effect on the outside world, feedback is a signal that comes back to the circuit and gives information about what kind of effect the circuit actually had.

Devices that make use of feedback can be far more accurate and "intelligent" than devices that simply take their best guess at what effect they're having. For instance, a Boeing 767 airplane with sophisticated electronic equipment can take off, fly from one airport to another, and even land without any human pilots steering the thing. It does it by making use of feedback: the computer on board takes its best guess at adjusting all of the controls to point the airplane where it wants to go. Then, many times per second, the airplane gets feedback from radio beacons, pressure gauges, and other instruments. The feedback tells the computer, "Hey, you're a couple of degrees off course from where you said you wanted to be." With that information, the computer adjusts the rudder, ailerons, or throttle with a new, more informed guess about how to get back on course.

The airplane spends almost all its time off course, but it doesn't matter: with the feedback, and the simple knowledge of where it wants to go, the computer makes course corrections so all the little errors don't add up.

For those of you who smelled an analogy coming, I won't disappoint you—because the concept of feedback applies exactly the same way to people.

> Whatever you want in life—whatever course you're on—making intelligent use of feedback can help you get closer to it, get it faster, and get more of it.

Feedback refers to any information that comes back to you about the effect you are having on the world. If someone compliments you on the clothes you are wearing, that's feedback. If your best friend takes you aside and whispers that you have bad breath (or even more subtly, offers you a mint), that's feedback. If you pass a coworker in the hall and smile at her, but she ignores you and walks right by, that's feedback. There don't even have to be other people involved: if you drive 50 mph down a slick, twisty road and spin out into a tree—you've just received some first-rate feedback on your driving.

We often hear about "positive" or "negative" feedback, but in reality feedback is nothing more than information. It's up to you whether you have positive or negative judgments about the information. If you let your judgments get in the way of really hearing the feedback, you won't be in a position to use it to help you get what you want out of life.

If you are serious about having the best life possible, you'll be hungry for every bit of feedback you can get. There are problems that are easy to solve, and problems that are hard to solve. But the problems that are *impossible* to solve are the ones you don't know about. Those are the ones for which listening to, and believing, feedback is invaluable. Because when we're really willing to face reality, problems tend to solve themselves.

BUT WHAT IF THEY'RE WRONG?

Feedback is just information. At one level, it can't be wrong. For instance, a policeman once lectured me for driving around his stopped car using the center two-way left-turn lane. He said I was not allowed to use the lane for passing, and I was lucky he didn't give me a $47 ticket. Although I thought that was ridiculous and neither appreciated his threat nor saw what was wrong with going around him, I determined to make use of the feedback. However, having a strong belief that it does no good to have prolonged discussions with policemen, especially if they've already decided *not* to give me a ticket, I decided to wait until later to make use of it.

*Receiving feedback from other people doesn't always
feel like the valuable learning experience that it is.*

To make good use of feedback, it's important to be clear about the difference between perceptions and conclusions. Perceptions are simply observations—scientific fact. There's no judgment, opinion, reaction, or conclusion involved. The story I told my friends about the incident, of course, was full of judgments, especially about the police officer. But if you leap right to your conclusions, you miss the most beneficial way to use feedback: finding unconscious patterns or beliefs that aren't helping you get what's most important to you.

The story I told my friends went something like this. I've put all my judgments and conclusions in *italics,* and left my perceptions and observations in normal type:

> I was driving down Broadway, *minding my own business,* when a police car *paid for by my tax dollars had nothing better to do than* stop right in front of me *to hassle* some taxi driver who was parked in a bus stop. I waited *forever for them to move,* then I *finally* pulled around them in the center lane *that everybody uses to go around stopped cars.* This cop *with a stick up his butt forgot all about the taxi driver,* flipped on his lights, and pulled me over! He *orders* me *in an incredibly condescending way* not to ever use the center lane, because it's only for left turns and police cars, and he *goes off on a power trip and* says I'm lucky I didn't get a ticket! *There's nothing wrong with going around a stopped car, is there? Wouldn't you have done the same thing?*

Notice how I cleverly jumped from the facts to the conclusions in this story. I believed the policeman was wrong, and attempted to get my friends to back me up. But the *feedback* was not wrong.

Feedback can never be "wrong" —
it is just information.

So what was the feedback here, anyway? There was the simple, verbal feedback from the police officer that my driving was in violation of the law. But beyond that, there was far more important information for me if I chose to look at it: something about the way I behaved that morning generated an unusually hostile response from a policeman.

Without separating perceptions from conclusions, there wouldn't have been much to learn from the feedback. Whether or not the policeman was right about the traffic law wasn't particularly important to me. But if there was something I was doing unconsciously to anger policemen—that was something I wanted to know.

If someone gives you feedback, and you don't want to hear it because you believe they're wrong, find the level at which they're right. It will be at the level of their perception. If the feedback they give you is more in the nature of a conclusion than a perception— "You've been a real bonehead lately"—the way to turn that into useful information is to ask what, in particular, they have noticed about you that would lead them to that conclusion. The less defensive and more genuinely curious you are, the easier this will go. Keep going until you get to a specific behavior that you understand:

"You've been a real bonehead lately."
"I have? Are you serious?"

"Yes. I'm at the end of my rope with you."
"Wow! I didn't realize I was having that effect on you. What am I doing that makes you think I'm a bonehead?"

"Whenever we're with a group of people, you treat me like dirt."
"I do? I had no idea—I certainly don't *want* to treat you like dirt. What is it I do that makes you feel like I treat you like dirt?"

"You just pay attention to them and not to me."
"Oh. Huh. Well, thanks for letting me know, because I wasn't aware I was doing that at all. If you wouldn't mind telling me, I'd really like to know—what in particular is it that I do that makes you feel like I'm paying attention to them instead of you?"

"You don't include me in the conversation."

"Oh. I've never thought of that. For me, the conversation just kind of has a life of its own and I'm not actively trying to include or exclude *anyone*. But you're saying you want me to include you more."

"Just give me a chance to say something once in a while. I feel like you talk right over me."

"Aha! I talk right over you! So that's what I do! You know, I think you're right. My conversational style is to jump in whenever I can so I can get my point across, and I probably talk right over you. That's really good to know—I bet there are lots of other people who get upset when I do that, too. I'll work on being more sensitive. Thank you."

CHECK IT OUT

When you get feedback that surprises you—meaning it doesn't fit in with your view of yourself—you have a choice about what to do with the information. You can accept it, believe it, and change your view of yourself to incorporate the new knowledge. (I smell bad? Huh! That's really hard to hear, but I believe she's telling me the truth, and if I smell bad to her, I probably smell bad to other people, too. Where's that deodorant?) Changing your view of yourself to be a closer match to reality often leads to an automatic solution to the problem.

If you're not ready to believe the feedback, either because you consider its source unreliable or because you doubt anyone else sees you the same way, I suggest checking around with some people you trust and asking them if they've ever noticed the same thing. For this to work, you've got to make it clear to them that you really want to hear the truth; you are unlikely to get any useful feedback with a set-up like, "Some jerk just told me I smell like the elephant cage at the zoo—can you believe them?"

In this case, I asked three of my friends what there was about me that would cause a policeman to get upset with me for driving around him. Here were the responses I got: "You tend to be intimidating sometimes." "I think he probably felt you were stepping on his toes." "You have this thing about challenging authority." Ouch! I checked it out, and what I thought was a completely inappropriate piece of feedback from the police officer turned out to give me new insight into the way other people saw me.

Because looking back on it, I didn't tell the whole story. There are many different ways to pull around a stopped car. The way I chose involved perhaps a bit more acceleration and jerking of the steering wheel than necessary. And I didn't exactly wait "forever" for the policeman to move; it was probably more like three seconds before I floored the accelerator and burned rubber. And, now that I think about it, I did feel a little bit of a power thing going on between the officer and me. Just a little.

After I let the initial hurt fade from hearing my friends' feedback, I had to admit that a "thing about challenging authority" fit me pretty well.

INCORPORATING FEEDBACK

The hard part about feedback is hearing it in the first place. Once you get it, believe it, and accept that that's how at least some people see you, that information will work for you automatically. The whole idea is that the more clearly you see yourself, the better equipped you are to go from where you are to where you want to be.

If there are people or situations you're avoiding because you just *know* there's some unpleasant feedback coming—just think how much mental energy it takes, and how bad it feels, to keep that crisis just at arms length rather than dealing with it. Not only do you have yet another fear, another piece of life to avoid, another undone—

but you also miss out on potentially valuable information that could help you improve the quality of your life. Get that feedback as soon as possible!

One excuse people use to justify not asking for feedback is they *already know* what the feedback is going to be. They don't have to ask—they've read the other person's mind. What a great trick! But remember, the most valuable feedback you get is going to be the feedback that surprises you: it's the time when you *just know* what the other person is thinking, and it turns out to be something else entirely.

> If you *just know* what someone's thinking and feeling about you, and you suspect it's unpleasant feedback, check it out. Ask anyway. Some of the most useful feedback comes when you ask about something you *just know*, but you're surprised by the answer.

Mind-reading isn't always accurate. You'll have greater success if you're willing to ask for, and listen to, feedback.

It's well worth the initial few minutes of discomfort to hear an important piece of feedback that you don't yet believe. Feedback provides the key to solving many of the frustrating, imponderable problems in life. Any time you feel like you're doing your best, but you're just not getting the results you want—maybe you see other people getting better results than you and you just don't see why that should be—a little bit of feedback can be the clue you need to get better results. It may not even take extra work—in fact, many times I've received feedback that resulted in my doing *less* work and getting better results. The important thing is to understand, and accept, the way others see you.

The feedback I got from the police officer, which was kindly corroborated by my three friends, helped me become more sensitive to the effect I had on other people. I have always been passionate about my convictions, and have never been reluctant to challenge authority when I felt it was acting unfairly. What I didn't realize is that what I had considered clear, emphatic statements of my position, other people saw as intimidating, threatening, or hostile shows of power. I learned people saw me as a lot more powerful than I saw myself. With that new knowledge, I gradually shifted toward more low-key statements of my convictions, and became more concerned with letting people know I respected and appreciated them in spite of our differences. As you might have guessed, that approach not only improved my relationships with people, but also made me much more effective at communicating my beliefs.

TALKING

Since I've already told my story about being caught lying to my dad, I won't dwell on the value of honesty here. I will point out, however, that unless at least one of the parties involved is telling the truth, not a whole lot gets accomplished even by years of communication. So let's assume, for the purpose of this chapter, you've decided to be honest, forthcoming, and truthful in your communication.

What would be some reasons for *not* telling the truth to someone? I had two main fears that kept me from being honest: the fear that someone would discover something bad about me and disapprove or reject me, and the fear that I would hurt someone's feelings by letting them know what I really thought of them. These were both very, very hard for me to overcome. So there had to be something very valuable for me to get me past those fears. There was, in fact, something that valuable: the quality of my life.

Failure to communicate was one of the main ways I built up stress in my life—stress in the form of guilt, resentment, and unresolved issues. So it made sense that communicating was a great way to turn that around and relieve the stress. The trouble was, when I felt guilty about something, I was afraid to tell anyone about it! There was that fear again, getting in my way. But knowing that many of the decisions I have made out of fear have been poor ones, I decided to do it anyway, at least a little, and see what happened.

Bit by bit, and with very safe people at first (for me "safe" meant a workshop setting with a group of strangers), I let my cats out of their bags. Each time I told someone one of these "secrets" I had kept bottled up, it was like my head had been held underwater and I finally could come up for air. What a relief!

As you may have guessed, people's reactions to what I considered major skeletons in my closet were far more understanding and forgiving than I had feared. Of course, I *picked* people I thought would be understanding and forgiving, but if you've ever been on the receiving end of one of these confessions, you know that these things are usually not that big a deal to anyone other than the one confessing. In fact, I realized that I was far more ready to forgive the human failings of *people I didn't even like* than I was to forgive myself for being less than perfect.

What does it say about me if I think there are things about me that are so awful that people would run in terror if they found out? It says there are some things about myself I really don't accept. Since the whole premise of this section is that when I increase my self-acceptance, I automatically improve my quality of life, I had a problem. As long as I had things about myself that I thought were so awful I couldn't tell *anyone*, I had a major lack of self-acceptance. So I decided to take the risk. I not only didn't lie, but I started actively telling the truth.

The major value in being actively honest, though, was not in airing out my dirty laundry. The main benefit came day to day, in being honest about what I preferred, rather than automatically agreeing to things I didn't want; in asking people for things I wanted, rather than waiting silently and hoping I would just get them; by letting people know who I really was and what was most important to me, rather than an image of someone I thought people would like.

Over and over, I was astonished: when I set my image aside, exactly the opposite of what I thought would happen actually did. People liked me *more.* They approved of me *more.* They wanted to be with me more, include me more in their lives. And then it occurred to me—maybe my image had been easier to see through than I thought. Once I let it down, and exposed my genuine self— even with my flaws—people saw someone much more attractive and genuine than they did before. I thought I was putting on a bang-up image, but other people didn't. Of course, I never thought to ask them for feedback.

THE TRUTH CAN HURT

Although setting my image aside and showing my real self was scary, by far the hardest thing for me to do was let people know what I really thought about them, what I wanted from them, or how I felt about what they wanted from me. I spent years and years in both working and personal relationships without ever suggesting that my employer or friend change something to please me. Of course, they asked me to do things and change all the time! For some reason, I didn't see the symmetry in the relationships.

From time to time, I would object to something if I was on solid ground that it was clearly inappropriate, like asking me to do something that wasn't part of my job description. Even when that happened, though, I got angry, self-righteous, and defensive. I was very uncomfortable speaking up.

My relationships, business or personal, never worked well until I started blowing my own horn—not in a demanding way or as an ultimatum, but simply voicing what I wanted in the relationship, giving feedback as to how I felt about things that were going on, and believing I had just as much right to create the structure of the relationship as the other party.

Now, this is not a license to be a jerk! I'm not saying to walk up to strangers and say, "You know, you and me being in the same room just isn't working for me. Not only do I have hemorrhoids, but I find you hideously ugly. I wasn't going to tell you, but I just read this great book—" My purpose in this chapter is to promote *effective* communication. Communication is a tool, like a hammer—please don't hit people over the head with it!

So when would it be appropriate to risk "hurting someone's feelings" and let them know what you really think? The easy answer is, when you have a genuine intention to help either them or yourself, rather than hurt. However, since people are not always open to feedback, even if you have the best of intentions, I would suggest you make sure they want to hear it before you give it. If there's any doubt—ask! Since I believe that listening to feedback is one of the easiest and most powerful ways for me to raise my quality of life, in many of my relationships I give people blanket permission to give me feedback any time they want to. And I listen.

15

◆

Commitment

The secret of success is constancy to purpose.
                              —Benjamin Disraeli

*Life is like a sewer: what you get out of it depends on what
you put into it.*
                              —Tom Lehrer

This section has been about your own personal liberty: different
ways to look at things, ways to get unstuck, tools to help you free
yourself to get what you want out of life. I sincerely hope you do.

So what's this word "commitment" doing in a section on Liberty? And not just mixed in with some other words, but sitting right
there by itself at the top of the page. A whole *chapter* on commitment?

If I had read this book ten years ago, this would have been the hardest chapter for me to swallow, no contest. It's tough to argue, for instance, with the idea of self-reliance, once you think about it. And things like honesty, power, and keeping agreements sound like pretty good goals for most people, even if they don't seem easy to achieve. But *commitment* — to many people that sounds less like liberty and more like the slamming shut of prison doors! I think most people would have no trouble giving a brief, unrehearsed half-hour presentation on why *not* to make commitments.

Many people are more familiar with the
disadvantages of commitment than with its advantages.

Shall we just bring it out into the open? I'll say it: "Commitment is *confining!* It's a ball and chain! I like to keep my options open. Why should I make up my mind now? What if something better comes along? I don't like to be tied down! Freedom is very important to me. I've committed before and been burned. Oh, no, I mean *really* burned. You don't even know how burned I'm talking about! And I'm not going to make *that* mistake again. Besides, they won't commit—why should I? You know—I don't even *like* committed people. They bug me. I think they're fanatics, or something. My philosophy is just take life as it comes, ride with the tide, move with the groove, run with the sun. Walk around me; what do you see? No strings."

If you have more issues with commitment, feel free to add to the ones I've just enumerated. And, by the way, if you notice any of your favorite reasons, excuses, or justifications coming up as you think about commitment, feel free to add them to your Excuses list.

If you share any of the above sentiments about commitment, you'll be glad to know this chapter is *not* about asking you to make new commitments. It's about understanding what a great tool commitment can be in your pursuit of a great life, and about clarifying those commitments that you already have made in your life.

WHAT IS COMMITMENT?

A commitment is a conscious choice to live your life with some sort of structure—to make a choice today about how you will live in the future. A commitment doesn't have to be an absolute, no-matter-what type of thing; it's just some form of conscious choice about your life. As long as you're clear about your choice and honest with yourself about your intentions, it's a commitment. You can have levels of commitment, ranging from least to most committed, as illustrated by these examples:

- I am going to play it by ear in my relationship with Alphonse.
- I am committed to go to the Bodybusters Club every day at 6:45 a.m. for an aerobic workout, if I feel like it.
- I am committed to obey the traffic laws unless I'm in a hurry.
- I am committed to work on my book at least an hour a week, every week, until I consciously decide to abandon the effort.
- I am committed to finish this project at work, no matter what other opportunities or greener pastures present themselves.
- I am committed to love, support, respect, and understand my wife, no matter what, as long as we both shall live.

If you're like me, you've looked at things in terms of "want to," "should," "have to," or "supposed to," and never in terms of what you are *committed to* do. Committed doesn't mean you have to: it means you chose to, and you're sticking with your decision.

What's the value of making a commitment? It allows you to make a decision when you have a clear head or strong gut feeling about the value of something, and then go ahead and follow through on it without wasting time and energy on any of the traps that come with being uncommitted: worrying if you should quit because you might fail, indecisiveness, checking out greener pastures, wondering if you're on the right track, and so on.

Now, commitment does not guarantee success! You *might* fail; there *might* be greener pastures; you *might* be on the wrong track. That's the downside. So when you make a commitment, make it be your best educated guess at what's right for you. Because by making a commitment, you will be eliminating some of your options in life. It'll be your choice, but you'll still be eliminating some options.

Of course, what I never realized before I discovered the value of commitment was that by *not* committing, I was also eliminating options—and in fact, over and over again, I missed out on much more happiness, success, and delight in my life by *not* committing than the reverse. If you don't believe me, try it.

RULES, POLICIES, AND LAWS

Let's start our examination of the commitments you already have in your life by looking at your level of commitment to the various rules, policies, and laws in your life. Remember, I'm not telling you that you should commit to obey every rule! I just want you to be conscious of the choices you are making.

People often feel as if there are a lot of "rules" in life. As adults, we really make our own rules by choosing which rules we are going to follow. Making conscious commitments about the structure of our lives gives us freedom, clarity, and focus to have the kind of lives we want. If you're committed to following a particular rule, then follow it because you're choosing to. If you're not, then don't waste any energy worrying when you break it, and be accountable for the consequences if somebody catches you.

I knew one man who often drove between Los Angeles and Las Vegas over a stretch of straight, lightly traveled freeway. He was not in any way committed to the 55-mph speed law, believing that it was safe and advantageous for him to travel 85 or 90 mph on that road, and considering that his time was more valuable than the cost of the traffic tickets he often received. Rather than resenting the existence of the law and being upset when he got caught, he considered the fine a "fast driving tax," which he was perfectly willing to pay for the privilege of getting there faster.

What rules or laws, if any, are you absolutely committed to honor, even with your life on the line? Which ones are you committed to honor unless, say, your life is at stake? To honor unless you see a tremendous benefit in breaking them? To honor if you don't think of a good reason why not? And which rules do you not even consider to apply to you—they wouldn't even be factors in making a decision?

Here are some examples of rules, policies, and laws. What is your level of commitment to these and others?

- Thou shalt not kill.
- Thou shalt not commit adultery.
- Thou shalt not violate any state or federal felony laws (bank robbery, blackmail, forgery, and so on).
- Thou shalt not drive while under the influence of drugs or alcohol.
- Thou shalt keep thine agreements with other people.
- Thou shalt make a fair and accurate accounting of thine income to the Internal Revenue Service so that they may tax thee properly.
- Thou shalt not violate any of thy company's policies as dictated in thine Employee Handbook.
- Thou shalt follow thy mother's advice, or at least feel bad if thou dost not.
- Thou shalt not drive faster than the speed limit.
- Thou shalt not cross the street in the middle of the block (jaywalk).
- Thou shalt keep thine agreements with thyself.

If the guilt and resentment are starting to set in, I'll say it one more time: *I'm not telling you that you should be committed to honoring these or any other rules.* I just want you to be conscious of where you stand right now on the notion of commitment, so that you can get the maximum value for yourself by using it as a tool. If this still sounds scary, just remember nobody can *make* you commit to anything. You get to choose. And I would highly recommend:

> Only commit to good stuff!

Are you pretty clear now about your level of commitment to various kinds of rules? Perhaps you resonate a little stronger with my statement above that, as adults, we really set our own rules. Be clear about how committed you are to each set of rules in your life.

Choose to honor the sets of rules that you, personally, are committed to—because you want the results that come from following them—and don't let the rest of them rule your life! Those results could be anything: from getting a promotion, to not having to worry about being thrown in prison, to simply feeling like a good citizen. The important thing is that you make your own choice.

Remember, being honest with yourself automatically increases your potential for having a great life; so I invite you to continue getting a clear picture of the existing commitments in your life.

COMMITTED RELATIONSHIPS

Life is full of relationships. Besides your Big, Meaningful Relationship with your spouse or other partner-for-life, if you have one, consider the relationships with your friends, parents, children, coworkers, and so on. What kinds of commitments do you have in each relationship? For example:

- I am committed to stay together no matter what.
  (Make sure that's really what you mean!)
- I am committed to be there in a time of crisis, unless it would cause serious problems for myself or others to do so.
  (This is a pretty honest statement of my level of commitment in many of my relationships.)
- I am committed to stay in touch for the rest of our lives.
  (Lifelong friends!)
- I am committed to keep the lines of communication open, even if I have to do it all myself, for as long as we work together.
  (Committing to this makes for effective working relationships. Make sure you mean it!)
- I am committed to provide financial support until they turn 18.
  (This is separate from any *legal* obligation.)

- I am committed to do my best to make this
  relationship work until one of us decides to call it
  quits.
  (This kind of commitment in a non-permanent
  relationship works a lot better than the one-foot-in-
  one-foot-out kind.)

In a few of your relationships, you may find you have a very deep commitment; clarifying it can make decisions easier and make the relationship even more fulfilling for you. In many of your relationships, you may find you have no commitments at all—or perhaps a general commitment to treat people politely and with respect, but nothing specific to that person.

If you're like me, the relationships in which you have the highest level of commitment are the same relationships you find most fulfilling. If that's true for you, which came first: the commitment, or the fulfillment?

At one point in my quest to figure out how to have a great life, I got very curious about just what it would take for me to have a really fulfilling relationship. So I wrote down a list of all the relationships I could think of, and then across the top I wrote the names of different factors I thought might influence how much I enjoyed a relationship—factors such as excitement, honesty, spontaneity, stability, whether I was special to them, and so on. Almost as an afterthought, I added "commitment" to the list. Then, for each relationship, I checked off the factors that I judged that relationship to have, and ranked the quality of each relationship on a scale of one to ten. Finally I ran the whole thing through the Microsoft Excel spreadsheet program to do a statistical correlation for me.

The result stunned me so much I stayed up half the night correlating the statistics in different ways to see if I made a mistake— but the results were the same every time. By far the most important factor in the quality of my relationships was *how committed I was.* Not how committed the other person was; not whether we were both equally committed; just how committed *I* was.

That was the first time I ever saw any value in a committed relationship. I had always taken the approach that commitment was something to avoid until it was absolutely necessary, like you were going to have a baby or something. You know, you go out with somebody—uncommitted—for several years, and things just work so well the situation becomes an "insurmountable opportunity." It dawned on me that, unless I started at least to have commitment in the back of my mind when I began dating a potential mate, the relationship would never get to the point of my wanting a commitment.

When it came to relationships, I was a major victim: I was waiting for commitment to come and get me, rather than realizing it was my choice all along, kind of like Dorothy in *The Wizard of Oz*. All I had to do was click my heels together three times and say, "I actually want to marry one of the women I meet!" All this had never occurred to me. My style was more to leave the back door open no matter what, so I could make a quick getaway in case things got unpleasant. Of course, in a loving relationship, that was kind of like leaving the back door open in a house in the winter so that I could leave if it got too cold inside.

> The simple act of closing the back door makes it a lot warmer inside.

Six months later, I met the most delightful person I have ever known, and we married a year after that. It's the highest level of commitment I've ever had in a relationship and, not surprisingly, the most fulfilling relationship in my life.

> If you're unwilling to commit to a relationship because you haven't found one that's good enough yet—you may have the cause and effect reversed. Try increasing your commitment, and see if the relationship gets better.

When I say "increase your commitment," I just mean decide you're going to hang in there. You can do this in gradual stages. Start by making a commitment to work through issues, rather than thinking about leaving. Put all you've got into the relationship, just for today. Then, after a while, maybe make a joint commitment to stay together for a couple of months or a year. Marriage works great for Dana and me, but I'm not particularly promoting it for everyone. Trust yourself to know what you want, and cut through the fear to commit to it.

COMMITMENT TO OTHER "RELATIONSHIPS"

You can look at any area of your life—career, family, volunteer work, spirituality—as a kind of "relationship," and the same association between level of commitment and level of fulfillment often applies. Pouring your energy into a job you're not committed to is like pouring a pitcher of water onto a table with no glass to hold it. Your energy will just dissipate with very little effect or result.

Making, and honoring, a commitment is like building a structure to hold and direct your energy—like having a glass to hold the water. The simple presence of the commitment causes your energy to focus on what's most important to you—to work towards improving the quality of your life and doing what is most meaningful—rather than uselessly evaporate.

COMMITMENT TO YOURSELF

I said I wasn't going to tell you that you should make more commitments in this chapter. I'm not big on "should" in general—I look at things more in terms of what works and what doesn't work. But if I was going to allow myself just one "should" in life, this would be it:

> Make the commitment to have a great life.

By being true to your commitment to yourself, you will flourish; by committing to make your life be about what *you know in your heart* is most important, you serve others, too. Whatever your commitments to others, you will best honor them from the power and strength you gain by honoring your commitment to yourself.

Make the commitment to have the richest, the most fulfilling, the most worthwhile, the most meaningful life possible. Make that your most important commitment, and everything else will follow.

PART III

◆

THE PURSUIT
OF HAPPINESS

16

◆

The Key Question

What is your name?
What is your quest?
What is your favorite color?

—*The Bridge Keeper,*
"Monty Python and the Holy Grail"

I remember the first time I jumped, naive and unsuspecting, into a cold swimming pool. The shock hit my whole body at once, stripping away my warmth and sending me into a mild panic before I realized I would be OK and I had passed through the ordeal without any permanent physical damage. I remember a similar shock the first time someone asked me what I wanted to be when I grew up.

I was totally unprepared for the question. "What, you mean I have to decide now?" I thought. A kind of warm, fuzzy security was stripped away from me. My complacent feeling that I would always be taken care of, that my life would always be laid out in front of me like my twelve grades of school or my pajamas at night, got punctured for the first time. After that trauma, I made sure I had an answer ready in case anyone asked again: I'd say I was going to be a lawyer, because it seemed like an answer guaranteed to impress people. I never became a lawyer, but when it came to defending myself against that dreaded question I had my case sewn up.

CHILDHOOD AND ADULTHOOD

My parents did, in my judgment, a wonderful job raising me. They gave me lots of love, little criticism, some honest feedback, and approved of me wholeheartedly when I succeeded in school or, really, in anything I was interested in. But even with what most would consider a near-ideal set of parents—or perhaps because of them—I had difficulty making the transition from childhood to adulthood.

I define being an adult as knowing with certainty what you want, what you consider success, and what is best for you. A child is in a training process, learning through reward and punishment, approval and disapproval from parents and teachers. As an adult *your own* approval is most important to you. You get continuing feedback—from other people in the form of reward and punishment, approval and disapproval, and from your own successes and failures—but you know best what is good for you.

> Being an adult means *you* know best what is good for you.

We spend our childhood being trained to do what our parents and teachers approve of. But we can get so used to seeking other people's approval—so comfortable in that pattern—that we don't stop to realize there's another way to live life.

I was so good at figuring out what people wanted from me and devising ways to give it to them that I never took the trouble to think about what I wanted for myself. Most high-school graduations, mine included, are hardly an adequate rite of passage into adulthood. I had no ceremony or initiation to tell me I was through with the phase of my life in which I was being trained how to live and beginning the remainder of my life: living!

When you spend a whole life living for other people's approval it's not easy to figure out what you really wants for yourself. Our educational system doesn't provide the mental tools to think about that kind of thing; most of our education is devoted to acquiring facts and strategies for getting things done.

> The highest quality of life comes when you make your own self-approval more important than the approval of others—when you make what's most meaningful to *you* more important than what others expect of you.

"I don't know what I want. I wish someone would tell me."

STRUCTURES IN YOUR LIFE

As children, we had many different kinds of structures imposed on us as we grew up: school rules, table manners, bedtime, house rules, and so on. It was our job to figure out how those structures worked, and then how to have the best life we could within those structures. Depending upon the individual and the environment we grew up in, we came up with one or more strategies for living within those structures. Some common strategies are:

- Do what is expected of you quickly to get it over with or get the reward.

- Ignore undesirable demands on you, or generate some sort of distraction, until the demands go away.

- Make lots of friends so you can help each other get by.

- Carefully analyze exactly what is expected of you so you won't make a mistake and be punished.

The most powerful, successful people learn more than one strategy and use the strategy most effective at any given time. I guarantee you, though, all adults are experts in at least one strategy for succeeding within a structure. If we weren't, we wouldn't have made it this far.

Most people glide right through from childhood to adulthood without anyone telling them they now have the option to choose for themselves the structures in their lives. Some people know it: the ones who drop out of high school at 16, as soon as they're allowed to, know it. But many of us who have been doing a great job, getting decent or better results within the structures imposed upon us, never think to shift gears from what we've been doing our whole lives: what other people expect of us.

We may get consistent praise, approval, and promotions as we continue to do well at what is expected of us, and there's certainly nothing wrong with that. I personally am very fond of praise, approval, and especially promotions. I get a good feeling from doing a good job. But there's still a part of me that's not satisfied merely by doing a good job and being praised for it.

SETTLING, SHOPPING, AND REBELLING

People have different ways of choosing and participating in the structures in their lives. Some people settle on some pretty good structures—a pretty good job, a pretty good marriage, in a pretty good country—and spend their lives within them. They might be pretty satisfied, or they might spend every day wishing they were somewhere else. Either way, they've settled.

Others find unsatisfactory structures—a string of cruddy relationships, moving from one cruddy job to another, living in one cruddy, run-down hole-in-the-wall after the next—and spend their lives shopping for better ones. Sometimes people switch from settling to shopping, or vice versa. But what they're all doing is *living within externally imposed structures.*

In fact, even if I'm a rebel, and decide I'm going to break the rules and do the opposite of what is expected of me, I'm still sabotaging my life by buying into these external structures. Rebels are very clear about what they *don't* want—but a rebel still honors the rebelled-against structure, though more in the breach than the observance. If you're a rebel, you may not be happy to hear this, but despite any satisfaction you get from displeasing the rule makers, you're still wired into their system: you're just plugged into the negative terminal instead of the positive.

Now, I'm not running down all externally imposed structures. With all its flaws, I think the constitutional structure of the United

States makes a wonderful place for me to live. My point is not that it's bad to live within other people's structures, or even that you can't be happy doing so. My point is there's another choice besides settling, shopping, and rebelling—an exciting, incredibly powerful alternative:

> You have the option of creating your own structures in life.

Remember the contrasting mindsets of victim and accountability from Chapter 11? If I view life as something that *happens to me* by always seeking out external structure and doing what is expected of me, I'm being a victim, which greatly limits my power to have a great life.

If I choose accountability, I realize that I make the choices in my life, and from those choices come my results.

> One of the most important choices in your life—a choice that has tremendous impact on your results—is the choice of which structures, externally or personally created, you are going to honor.

How do you choose, let alone create, suitable structures to live your life by? I would suggest that, at a minimum, you get very clear about your answer to the Key Question hinted at by this chapter's title. That question is: "What do you want?"

Often, people confuse the answer to this question with a shopping trip through the "structure supermarket." They think maybe they would be happy if only they could find the right job, the right car, the right mate, the right place to live, the right political system, the right dog, the right brand of laundry detergent, and so on.

Not so.

HAPPINESS

I called this final section *The Pursuit of Happiness,* but when I talk about happiness, I mean more than just having fun—I mean the complete, rich sense of fulfilling everything that is meaningful to you, that you crave, that you delight in. I'm talking, in an abstract, essential sense, about the answer to the Key Question.

Perhaps you believe there is something special about human beings, something that gives us a greater capacity for delight, for agony, and maybe a greater responsibility to make full use of our lives than non-human animals have. Or you could believe something more along the lines of, "As long as I'm here, what else is there to do?" No matter what you believe about who you are, why you're here, or where you're going, the only thing that makes sense in life is to devote it to what matters most. And like it or not, the one who will be making the decision about what matters most is you.

What do you want? At this point you may be quite clear about it, or you may not have a clue. If you are quite clear, and some of your top priorities include things like "more money" or "work fewer hours," I'd like to challenge you to dig a little deeper and figure out what experience you're looking to have with the money or extra time—feeling more secure or relaxed, for example. If your top priorities are goals such as a promotion or a new house, dig a little deeper. What experience of life are you looking for? These are tough questions, but you must know with absolute certainty what is most important to you if you want to get it.

Goals are great. People who set goals get much more done than people who don't. I set goals all the time. When I write computer programs, my personal goals mesh together with those of my development team; those goals combine with those of other teams to form whole business unit goals, resulting in a beautiful, synchronized climax and shrink-wrapped boxes rolling off the assembly line. Goals work.

However, goals don't in themselves bring people a fulfilling, satisfying life. They may make you lots of money, which can give you great flexibility in the way you structure your life, but they won't bring you everyday fulfillment.

It is absolutely possible to create a situation where you enjoy life tremendously—where you wake up each morning looking forward to a day filled with fulfilling, satisfying, invigorating experiences. I have seen people from their teens to their nineties learn to create more joy, excitement, and happiness in their lives than they ever thought possible. In fact, I believe it would be possible to teach children how to create this for themselves as they grew—and probably be better at it than adults, as a native speaker is more fluent than one who learns a second language.

OK, so why doesn't everyone do this? It's not like it's tough to sell people on the idea of having more fulfilling lives! Why don't people know about this? Why can't Thoreau's "lives of quiet desperation" become the exception rather than the rule?

Beats me. Maybe this book will help. If all I accomplished in this book was to persuade people that having a life filled with fulfillment and delight was *possible* for them, I would consider all the work that went into it worthwhile. Because anyone who knows for sure that such a life is possible will do *whatever it takes* to get it.

17

◆

A Life Purpose

What is the answer?
[I was silent.]
In that case, what is the question?

—*Gertrude Stein,*
last words, to Alice B. Toklas

The first time I heard the idea of having an overall life purpose, I was more than a little skeptical. It smacked of being a missionary or religious zealot. I sniffed around the subject for a while and did all the work necessary to figure out what my life purpose would be, *if* I decided to commit to one, but I still held back. "Commit" was not my favorite word back then.

I'm trying to give you a sense of who I am in this book by writing about my own experiences in my own conversational style, and I hope at this point you've come to view me as a practical, common-sense kind of person. I'm interested in results. All the theories in the world bore me to tears unless they are about results. So what results can you expect from doing the work to figure out your life purpose and committing to it? Because, although the work involved is not particularly difficult—and many people find it fun and fascinating—it's a lot more work than simply reading a book.

Based on my own experience, you can expect to:

- Feel more powerful.
- Find that other people are much more willing to support you and believe in you.
- Be happier.
- Have much more of a sense of meaning and fulfillment.
- Be much more successful by your own and others' standards.
- Be more admired and attractive to others.
- Like yourself more.
- Be much less bothered by stuff that happens.
- Enjoy life more.

This is true whether or not you've had much success in your life thus far. If you haven't, the benefits of turning that around are obvious. If your life has already been a string of successes—well, *before* I committed to my life purpose, I had attended Harvard, made a million dollars, written one of the world's best-selling computer programs, and won a new car on the game show *Sale of the Century*. So please believe me:

> Even if you are already a wonderful person and a great achiever, you have an incredible amount to gain by working to discover your purpose.

Now remember—I'm not asking you to accept *my* purpose for you, or to adopt *my* belief system or values. I want you to *discover* the purpose *you already have* in your life. You can view this as deeply spiritual, or as simply clearing your head.

HOW CAN YOU BE SURE?

The one thing that always stopped me, as I grew up and occasionally pondered the question of what I wanted my life to be about, was the fear that, if I picked one thing to dedicate my life to, how would I know I made the right choice? It always seemed far safer to take small steps, just kind of doing what I knew how to do, until—

Until what? That was the problem. I've heard stories about people who got a clear "calling" in their life—people who "just knew" what the purpose of their life was. But after my first 20 or 25 years had passed with no booming voice out of the sky telling me my purpose, I suspected I'd better not count on that happening.

Many of the great thinkers throughout history have addressed the question of purpose in life. Not surprisingly, they don't all agree. Brilliant, eloquent, respected people from Socrates to M. Scott Peck have proposed different answers to that question. Some of the best knowledge-seekers of history have said the quest for knowledge is, in fact, the purpose of life. Some very creative people have proposed that the purpose of life is to create. Ernest Hemingway and Ralph Waldo Emerson, both distinguished, powerful individualists, each wrote a clear, powerful, individualistic statement of what it means to succeed in life. The two statements, of course, were different.

So how could I be sure? I took a good, hard look at the premise that I've made the foundation of this whole book—the advice that Shakespeare, Emerson, and my father all thought essential enough to argue for. I decided—rather than waiting for lightning to strike, rather than weighing and sifting through all the conflicting messages from others about what *should* be important to me—to rely on my own sense and judgment about what was meaningful in life.

I decided on self-reliance.

And—as Robert Frost and M. Scott Peck both found in taking the road less traveled by—it has made all the difference.

FILLING IN THE GAPS

It helped ease my fear to realize that I would not be making a major change in my life, but simply be identifying what I *already* wanted my life to be about, and just adding more of it—filling in the gaps.

Listen carefully: your purpose in life is to memorize every episode of "Gilligan's Island."

You could wait a long time for a booming voice to come out of the sky telling you your purpose in life—and even then, would you believe it?

The kind of life purpose I'm talking about is something that we are all fulfilling already; it's just that we may be doing it very inefficiently. I want you to become conscious of what that purpose is—the part of your life that you really like, the core of what it's all about for you—so you can use all your intellectual and creative abilities to come up with ways to have more of it. And if you're like me, it won't just be a little more—it'll be a *lot* more.

I had a lot of fun in my life and found much of what I did worthwhile before I discovered the value of being clear about my purpose. The problem was, I would stumble across some situation I truly enjoyed—it was fun, worthwhile, exciting, absorbing—and then, as happens in life, things changed and the situation gradually (or suddenly, sometimes) got tedious, boring, dull, stressful, or just plain painful. And I had no idea what went wrong, how to stop it, or how to find a new situation that would make my life as fulfilling as the old one.

That's why it's essential to be conscious of your life purpose. By knowing it consciously, you can easily get back on track when you get off. More importantly, you can use the knowledge to create new situations and structures in your life that support your purpose.

Not being conscious of your purpose is like groping around a library in the dark looking for something good to read. You may find a book, but you have no idea if you'll like it until you get it home and start reading. And even if you like it, once it's done, you're back in the dark looking for another one.

Knowing your purpose is like flipping on the lights—all of a sudden, not only can you see the titles and authors, but you also have access to the subject index and cross-references! It makes a lot better use of your time—and life.

Some people who don't know their purpose—or rather, aren't *conscious* of it, because my whole premise is that we do know it at some level—get tired of groping around in the dark and just read the same book over and over again once they find one that's acceptable. Trying unsuccessfully to recreate fulfillment by repeating old experiences is a common complaint of people before they get clear about purpose.

I want to make this sound exciting, because it is. From the many people whom I have personally encouraged to do the work to clarify their purpose, usually through seminars or workshops on the topic, the almost unanimous feedback I get is that doing that work was more valuable than they had ever imagined.

Why?

Think of the peak experiences of your life; the best times you've had; the most joyous times; times when you felt worthy, important, or delighted. Then imagine feeling like that *a lot more often*. It's not too much to expect to have that kind of experience in your life on a daily basis. And not by repeating those exact experiences—I'm not sure I'd be up for an encore performance of my Sixth-Grade play—but by understanding the core part of you that found meaning, fulfillment, and delight in those experiences.

That core part of you is your life purpose.

CAN YOU REALLY DISCOVER YOUR LIFE PURPOSE BY READING A BOOK?

You will not find your own, unique, individual life purpose actually printed in this book, of course. I have those in another book, for only $79.95: just call this toll-free number—only kidding. You need to discover it for yourself. I'll give you all the information I have about how to do it, but the rest is up to you.

You *already have* a personal sense of what is important, worthwhile, and meaningful in life. You already have feelings of joy, love, delight, and satisfaction. You already know which experiences, people, and things you find attractive and which you find repulsive or indifferent.

> Discovering your life purpose is as simple as finding the common denominator in what you already know.

For those of you who appreciate an overview of what you are about to do if you follow along with me in these next chapters: you're going to take a look at your answer to the Key Question "What do you want?" from several different angles; you're going to distill the essential elements from that; and you're going to roll the whole thing up into a statement of your life purpose.

The process of discovering your life purpose is a lot like solving a puzzle—for many people, the most fascinating puzzle of their life. No short-cuts here! You're the only one in the world who has the solution. If you're somewhat analytical, you may enjoy this process tremendously. If not—well, look forward to the results!

That process starts with the next chapter.

18

◆

Success

Everybody wants to feel good. In fact, there's one school of thought that says that's really all anybody wants. But there isn't just one "good feeling" that either you have or you don't: each of us can experience a broad spectrum of possible good feelings. They range from the simple physical pleasure of a friendly touch or a tasty snack to the deep, gut-level satisfaction of a job well done, helping someone in need, or making a difference in the world. While some of these good feelings come from meeting physical needs, others are something else. What?

Various philosophers and psychological researchers have categorized feelings into different classes and levels, something which I resist. But let's focus on those good feelings that relate to things such as fulfillment, satisfaction, joy, delight—something other than physical or survival feelings. This isn't anything profound; it's just that most people already understand how to meet physical needs such as hunger, drowsiness, and libido. I want you to know how to meet your fulfillment needs, too.

Like musical notes that make up a chord, or the various colors that, when combined, form white light, when all your fulfillment needs get met simultaneously, they combine to form a rich, full experience of life. Before I got interested in this stuff, I had a few peak experiences in my life in which many or all of my fulfillment needs showed up simultaneously. I felt great! Not just in the physical sense, but in the deep, blossoming, triumphant, top-of-the-world sense. Of course, these situations lasted for only a few hours or days at most, and when the feeling subsided, I had no idea how to get it back. I had no idea because I was not conscious of what my fulfillment needs were—I was not conscious of my *life purpose!*

> When you are living your life purpose effectively, all your fulfillment needs get met regularly in a constructive way.

YOUR SUCCESS CHECKLIST

Once you have your unique list of your own personal fulfillment needs—your "Success Checklist"—the next time something seems missing or empty in life, you can tick down the list to see what it is. It's one of those needs! When you are confronted with a difficult choice, you hold up your list of fulfillment needs in front of the possible scenarios like a filter, to see which choice fits the best.

166

The first step, then, in discovering your life purpose, is going to be to figure out what your fulfillment needs are. Because whatever your purpose is, it's going to be something that meets those needs.

I've heard some people express the concern that all this focus on meeting your own fulfillment needs is being selfish, and it's more appropriate to have a life purpose that's a bit more altruistic than that. I understand the concern. But while some of your fulfillment needs may seem selfish, especially at first, other needs are most likely directly related to the contribution you are making to others or to the world. And if you try, as many do, to deny yourself some of your needs and focus solely on the "altruistic" ones, you will not have as much energy to put into your altruism.

Your Success Checklist gives you a straightforward way
to improve your quality of life in any situation—
just look at each item on the list to see what's missing.

When you meet *all* your fulfillment needs, you feel confident, successful, and good about yourself, and you're generally an enjoyable person to be around. Who would *you* would prefer to be with: a happy, confident, fulfilled person or a noble, unhappy martyr?

If you're deeply committed to making a contribution to the world—and I'm not saying you *should* be—think about this: meeting *all* your fulfillment needs gives you the most energy and power to flourish and make your maximum contribution to the world. In the same way the colors of the rainbow combine to form white light, when you honor all parts of yourself and structure your life so you meet all your fulfillment needs, you shine with your own unique light and brighten the world. It also feels *great*.

Besides, denying that *any* of your needs exist, either because you find them selfish or for another reason, doesn't work very well. If you consciously try to deny one of your fulfillment needs, most likely it will squirt out in some other form unconsciously. And if you are truly "successful" and manage to get your unconscious not to meet that need either—well, then you'll just feel bad. For many people, "successfully" denying a fulfillment need results in a sense of emptiness or lack of meaning in life.

BACK TO THE KEY QUESTION

Now it's time to look at your answers to the Key Question. I would suggest getting a sheet of paper or a word processor and jotting things down as they occur to you. I'm going to ask the question several different ways, but there's no need to separate your answers right now. Just make a list of everything that comes to mind.

When you write down your answers, focus on the *experiences* you hope to have by getting what you want, rather than going into great detail about the physical characteristics of the thing. For example, if you wanted to compose a hit Broadway musical, you might write:

I want to compose a hit Broadway Musical, so people from all over would know who I was and admire me; I'd feel like I made my mark in the world; important people would treat me well; I'd get the special perks reserved for VIP's; I'd be able to hold free shows for children and feel like I was making a difference in their lives. With the money I would make, I could have tremendous freedom to do anything I wanted.

Notice there are only six words about the *thing* you want—"to compose a hit Broadway musical"—but many more about the *experience* you want. That's the whole idea here: we're trying to find the experiences in common with the things you want. So feel free to go on and on and on about feelings and experiences, but don't bother with details about physical things—we won't be using those.

Also, be honest. You don't ever have to let anyone else see this, but this is the time for you to own up to what you really want, even if you've been told your whole life it's not OK to want it. For instance, it's not hard to imagine being a bit embarrassed to admit that "getting the special perks reserved for VIPs" is something one might value. But if you withhold anything out of embarrassment, you'll deny yourself an important clue to one of your fulfillment needs. So tell yourself the truth, the whole truth, and nothing but the truth.

Also, any time "more money" or "more time" comes up in your work here, dig deeper to get a feel for the *experiences* you want to have with that money or time. Money and time are means to an end.

YOUR ANSWERS TO THE KEY QUESTION

If you're ready, it's time to get out your paper or word processor and write away. There is obviously no "right answer" to any of these questions; in fact, simply putting down whatever comes to mind will probably give you the most value from this exercise. But do hang in and take the time to search yourself a bit. Doing this exercise could take an hour or even several hours, so you may want to take steps to avoid being interrupted, although it's fine not to do it all at once. Remember, the emphasis is on *feelings and experiences.* And be true!

What do you want? Let's just start with the basics. Write down anything that you want in your life. These can be big things or small things. Remember, just a few words on the thing, then as much as possible on the experience. Come up with at least 10 things you want, and elaborate in great detail on the feelings and experiences you are looking for.

What have been the greatest successes of your life so far? These are successes by your own judgment, not necessarily other people's (although that's fine too). Start with the earliest success you remember. If you remember, write down the greatest success of each year of your life. Just write a few words about the event itself, then elaborate on your experience. How did you feel? What was it that made it feel like a success?

What is it about other people that you admire? Write down anything you see in other people that you admire. This can be personality traits, accomplishments, or anything else. What is it about the way they are treated that you would like to have for yourself? What experiences do you see them having that seem attractive to you?

What are some things you enjoy that don't fit into the mainstream of life? Write down activities that you go out of your way or off the beaten path to do, emphasizing, of course, what you like and how you feel about the experiences that go along with the activity.

What are your most important values? What ideals do you hold highest, honestly? Of notions such as honesty, wealth, love, integrity, passion, and beauty (but don't limit yourself to those!), which are truly most important to you?

What did you really enjoy doing as a kid at play? Describe the feelings and experiences from some of your most joyous moments as a child playing. Just a few words on the physical description, but elaborate on the experience.

Describe your ideal job. Go into detail about how you would feel, what experiences you would have, and how you would be treated.

Describe your ideal relationship. Again, go into detail about how you would feel and be treated. Be brief about what you would *do*, and elaborate on the *experience*.

Write about what life is like from the point of view of your favorite pet. If you don't have a pet, pick any non-human object or animal that pops into your head. Write about what life is like using "I," as if you were the pet or object. Do this one without thinking too much about it, please.

The Common Denominator

The next step is for you to look back over the list you've just made, and identify the words and phrases that come up in more than one or two places. Write these down on a new sheet of paper—don't worry about the order or about mixing different kinds of things; we'll sort that out in a bit.

The idea behind all that work was to peel back the first layer underneath the "doing" part of life, and to focus on the "being" that makes the doing worthwhile. I said before that I had wandered into several peak experiences in my life, and then wandered right back out because I was not conscious of what it took to make a peak experience for me. By looking at the set of feelings and experiences common to the things you want or have considered successes, you can begin to get conscious of the core set of experiences you personally require to have a "success."

So go ahead and make a new list of anything that stands out from the set of feelings and experiences you noticed when answering those different forms of the Key Question. At this point, it's better to have too much than not enough, so don't be afraid to put something down on the new list if it seems at all important. Make your new list now.

NEEDS, MEANS, AND STRUCTURES

The next step is to sort your new list—your list of feelings and experiences that you find fulfilling or associate with "success"—into three categories: needs, means, and structures. To help you do that, I'm going to explain what I mean by those three categories.

One of my survival (not fulfillment!) needs is oxygen. The means I use to get it is breathing. I have this great setup I call "the atmosphere" full of air that I breathe. The *need* is oxygen; the *means* is breathing, and the *structure* is the whole apparatus from my lungs to the Earth's atmosphere.

I'm guessing it didn't take long for early scientists to realize people needed to breathe. People are pretty good at identifying the *means* by which they're meeting their needs. But it took a lot longer to discover that one of the *needs* we were filling through the *means* of breathing was the intake of oxygen. As soon as people discovered the fact that all we *needed* was oxygen, and that we were not locked into the particular *structure* of breathing fresh air, we opened up a whole new set of possibilities: scuba diving, space travel, even oxygen-rich air for emphysema patients.

> The key to opening up possibilities is discovering the *core need;* with that knowledge, it is relatively easy to set up new *means* and *structures* to fill the need.

172

Your fulfillment needs work the same way. But while survival needs, such as oxygen, are the same for every human being and animal—although fish, for instance, use different *means* to get it than we do—your basic fulfillment needs are unique to you.

Your complete Success Checklist will only have *needs* on it—no structures, no means—because means and structures come and go, but your core fulfillment needs are yours forever.

So, one more time: a *core need* is one of the feelings or experiences that is essential for you, a unique individual, to have success or fulfillment in your life. When things are going fantastically well, all your *core needs* are present for you. You may have one or more *means* of getting a *core need* filled. You may just stumble into and out of situations where the need gets filled, or you may have one or more *structures* set up in your life to help fill it.

Often, it can be difficult to tell the difference between a *means* and a *core need*. Two years after I created my own personal Success Checklist, I actually realized that three of the items I had on it were not core needs at all, but in fact different means of filling another need that I didn't even have on my list. When I realized that, I crossed off the three means and added the new need. Sometimes the means look very much like core needs; it just takes peeling back layer after layer until you arrive at the core.

How do you know if you've got it? It just clicks. My own personal experience, and what I've heard repeatedly from people who've created their own Success Checklist, is that each *core need* just clicks into place—you know when it's right. And you know when you have a complete list, too. People often "fine-tune" their list or peel back some layers of means to reveal underlying core needs, but when your Success Checklist clicks for you, chances are that you've got the essence of it.

To get you familiar with the process of peeling back layers from structure to means to core need, this table gives some examples from the lives of some made-up people. Of course, your checklist is different and unique! And a given structure or means can fill completely different core needs for two different people. Remember, these are only examples. If you hang out in bars and flirt, it may be filling very different needs for you than it was for our made-up friend. Some people drive fast because they like the excitement; some people just want to get where they're going. Take the time and spend the effort to discover your own core needs.

Structure	Means	Needs Filled
High-paying job as an engineer	Make a lot of money	Independence Being important Recognition
	Solve difficult technical problems	Discovery Challenge Accomplishment
Go for walks in the woods	Get peace and quiet in nature	Beauty Serenity Connection
Hang out in bars and flirt	Get attention from opposite sex	Feel attractive Feel special Feel wanted
	Act aloof	Superiority

CRAVINGS

I want to talk about one more thing before I turn you loose to take a crack at completing your Success Checklist. That is the notion that some of your most powerful fulfillment needs—some of the most important parts of who you are at the core—may be cloaked in the disguise of a means or structure that you don't like very much.

Some fulfillment needs are so strong that whatever experience generates them has to be present absolutely all the time, all day long. These very strong needs are like cravings. If you consciously disapprove of one of these cravings and try to deny it, or even if you don't deny it but simply haven't structured your life in such a way as to meet it constructively, your unconscious will work like mad to find some way to meet it.

Since this gets done without your conscious approval, it's likely that the way your unconscious picks will be counterproductive to some other needs or somehow destructive to your life. For instance, my not being conscious of some of my cravings years ago led to some destructive patterns and major stress in my job. Not knowing what those cravings—or any of my core needs—were, I had no idea how to structure my life to meet them, and my unconscious started pulling me in all kinds of different directions in a desperate attempt to meet those cravings.

Several years after I quit that job in an attempt to relieve the stress, I did the work to construct my Success Checklist. That tool was so useful to me that, had I known back then, I could have completely avoided the stress, humiliation, and financial loss that came with the whole episode. I could *easily* have made some minor changes in the structure of my job to honor those cravings in a constructive way, and made myself and everyone involved a lot happier. But I didn't know.

If this business of honoring cravings in a constructive way sounds contradictory—if the word "craving" sounds inherently destructive to you—please bear with me, because this is one of the most important points of everything I have learned:

> The craving that most drives you to harm yourself or others is the same craving that will motivate you to greatness. It is only the *expression* of the craving, not the craving itself, that helps or hurts.

The craving I filled as an 11-year-old by being the pitcher on my Little League team (and throwing a temper-tantrum when the coach moved me to right field) is the same craving I fill when I give a talk in a room filled with people, and the same craving I fill when I work on a new computer program with the potential to make a breakthrough in the way people do office work.

If I try to suppress this craving because I don't like one means of filling it—temper-tantrums—all that does is drive my unconscious to find other ways to express it. If, on the contrary, I become conscious of the craving and look for constructive ways to feed it, I can use it to motivate myself to do great things in life.

That's why it doesn't work to focus only on the "noble" elements of your life purpose—those cravings are a part of your life purpose, too, because with them comes your motivation in life. The trick is to separate the cravings themselves from the harmful expressions of them. The cravings are *core needs;* the harmful expressions are (not particularly productive) means of filling those needs.

TAKE A CRACK AT IT

You are now ready to take a crack at constructing your Success Checklist. Go over the work you've done here, analyze all the feelings, experiences, needs, structures and means that have shown up in your answers to the Key Question, and come up with your list of core fulfillment needs.

It will take you at least several hours of real thought to get all your core needs to click into place. When I did this, I got a good, if rough, list in several hours, and kept tinkering with it for about two years, but 90% of the value was in those first several hours. You may want to think about it, sleep on it, then return to the task the next day. If you take this seriously, it will be among the most valuable several hours you ever invest in your life.

If you're panicking, don't. The worst that can happen right now is you make only a *little* progress toward having more fulfillment in your life instead of a *lot.* You don't have to turn this in. You can keep working on it as you go through life: when something feels like success, ask yourself what needs you are filling. When things aren't working, ask yourself what needs are missing. There's no pressure. It's just life.

So go for it! Take your best shot at creating your Success Checklist!

19

◆

Fulfillment

*I am putting myself to the fullest possible use, which is all,
I think, that any conscious entity can hope for.*
                            —HAL, "2001: A Space Odyssey"

If you've survived the process of exploring your fulfillment, and now have your own personal Success Checklist, congratulations! You now have an opportunity to join the elite group of people who have decided to do more with their lives than just survive. You now have the opportunity to commit to your purpose in life.

What is your purpose in life? Essentially, you've already answered that question. When you created your Success Checklist, you included all the elements that make life a success for you—not only those things that are fun and exciting, but also the things you consider important, worthwhile, and meaningful.

> Your Success Checklist contains all the elements of your purpose in life.

Now that you know what's most important to you, why not make a commitment to live by it? Simply by being conscious of your Success Checklist—do memorize it, by the way—you'll automatically increase your level of fulfillment in life. Committing to your life purpose will clarify the direction you are headed in and increase your rate of progress—maybe a little, maybe a lot.

If you want to commit to your life purpose, think about what that involves. It means making decisions in each area of your life with the goal of filling all your core needs constructively as often as possible. It means making what's most important to you, as outlined in your Success Checklist, more important than fear, other people's approval, inertia, excuses, reasons why not, and so on. It means changing the structures in your life, or perhaps adding new ones, to support all your core needs.

And most of all, it means realizing you must rely on yourself to fill those needs in each area of your life. Life isn't about shopping (unless shopping fills your core needs!). No matter how long and hard you shop for the perfect orange, you still have to peel it, open it up, and chew it yourself.

A PURPOSE STATEMENT

To assist you in committing, I suggest you come up with a statement of your purpose in life. If you like, it could be something simple, like

"My purpose in life is to have as full and worthwhile a life as possible, according to my Success Checklist."

Or you may want to play around with the items on your Success Checklist, and kind of roll them all up into an image that serves as your purpose statement. For example, if your Success Checklist contained "speed, beauty, leading, creating, and marching in step," you might decide, "My purpose in life is to be First Trombone in the Marching Band of Shangri-La." (You might be a very interesting person to get to know.) If you're a deep, serious person, make your purpose statement deep and serious. If not, don't! Just make something that's honest and works for you.

Being one who loves to keep my options open, I went with the first style for a few years, then switched to the more creative one when I thought of a good one. But my underlying *commitment* to my purpose never changed; just the wording.

So come up with a statement of the purpose of your life that you're willing to commit to and, when you're ready, make a formal commitment. You know, say it out loud, and light a candle, have a toast, beat a drum or something. A commitment to making the most of your life deserves a little ceremony, don't you think?

WHAT NOW?

Well, now you've done it. If you've just committed to your life purpose, things will look different from now on. Excuses won't work any more; you're either living your Success Checklist or you're not. So, if you're not, what does that mean?

It means you have an incredible new tool for improving any situation you find yourself in. Any time you feel like you're bored, frustrated, wasting your time—anything less than fulfilled—go through your Success Checklist and find out which items are missing. Remember, you're committed—so really do it! Other things are not as important as your commitment to your purpose in life. At first, you may find yourself often having to decide whether keeping your commitment to your life purpose is worth:

- Changing from the way things are now.
- Risking other people's disapproval.
- Changing your mind about some old attitudes or opinions, rather than proving you're right.
- Getting past fear.
- Risking and resolving conflicts.

If you want different or better results in life, you're going to have to change. It's OK to keep all the parts of you that you like. Just change the parts that are getting in your way.

Some people may resent you for changing, or simply for having a great life when they don't, no matter how nice or generous you are to them. You're not hurting them in any way, but they will still disapprove of you. You'll need to decide whether you're willing to give up on your purpose in life in order to please those people.

Many of the changes you make may be changes in your context—letting go of some old attitudes and opinions, even beliefs,

"I like all the stuff about improving my quality of life— just tell me how to do it without changing anything."

that were not supporting you in living your purpose. I remember letting go of the belief that I shouldn't have a business relationship with my best friend, because mixing business and pleasure just doesn't work. Hah! When we found the opportunity to work together in a situation that looked like it would be a great fit with both of our life purposes, I swallowed hard, changed my mind about that belief, and went on to have the most enjoyable job I've ever had. Now the fact that I probably *got* that belief from watching some TV show when I was six didn't matter; it was still difficult to let go. My clear focus on living my life purpose allowed me to make a good decision and free myself of a limiting belief.

Changing your ways can be scary. But remember, people have a lot more fear than the little bit we need to keep us safe from harm. As long as there's no physical danger involved, chances are moving in the direction of your life purpose is a better decision than giving in to the fear. Fear that keeps you from doing what's most important to you is just an illusion; it's a message from your DNA that it wants you to stay safe so that you can make lots of copies of it rather than getting eaten by a saber-tooth tiger. Treat that unwanted fear as an annoying advertisement for a product you don't want or need: you can watch it, notice it's there, completely ignore it, and do what you were going to do anyway.

YOU CAN ALWAYS LIVE YOUR PURPOSE

Remember all that work to peel away the layers of structures, means, and experiences, leaving only the core needs? We did that so *you can always live your purpose.*

> Every core need is something that you can *always* get filled somehow.

If we just had a checklist of structures and means—"work at Microsoft, have a front-wheel-drive car, be married to Dana, and own all the latest gadgets"—what happens when I do all that, and I'm still not satisfied? I have no place to go! Or what happens if they stop making front-wheel-drive cars?

No, the value of having only core needs on your Success Checklist is that when something is missing, it's easy to figure out what it is. You just run down the list until you find the ones that are missing. Once you know what they are, you have several options. For example, if one of my core needs is "beauty" and it's missing from my job as a garbage collector, I could:

1. Figure out a means of getting the need met within the existing structure of my job: mount some beautiful art prints inside the cab of my truck.
2. Figure out a way to modify the structure of my job to provide more of the need: ask to be transferred to a route in a nice wooded area of the city.
3. Change the way I *look at* my job to see the beauty I create by cleaning up the garbage.
4. Get a new job in an art museum, assuming it's an attractive way to get more of my core needs met easily.

Note that "resent my job and wait for the people I work for to meet my needs for me" was *not* on the list. Resentment doesn't produce much change. And being accountable for meeting your own needs is the most effective way to get them met.

GREENER PASTURES

I recommend putting a fair amount of energy into solutions 1-3 before considering number 4. There is a tendency people have, when things aren't going so well in some area of their life, to view alternative situations in a somewhat optimistic light. This is known as the myth of *greener pastures*. It applies to jobs as well as personal relationships, and often leads to the shopping syndrome: going from job to job, or person to person, shopping for one that will meet all our needs without us having to do any work ourselves. I'm not sure any jobs or people like that exist, at least after we leave the womb. So a word of advice:

> Your commitment to your life purpose is *not* an excuse to break other commitments in your life!

If you have an existing commitment to a job or relationship, number 4 above is not an option. So it's a good thing there are any number of ways to meet each core need—you just need to get creative. Even if your commitment to purpose is the most important thing in your life, take your best shot at making it work within your existing commitments before you decide to abandon them. If you get stuck, brainstorm with your friends. They don't even need to have read this book: if I went to a friend and asked, "Do you have any ideas how I can get more beauty into my life?" they would understand. When you break a commitment, it hurts you.

There's an added benefit to hanging in and finding new means to fill your core needs—even if you're not at all committed to staying in the situation or relationship:

> Every time you learn a new way to fill one of your core needs, you can use that way again and again, for the rest of your life.

The more effort you devote to finding ways to meet your needs within the existing structures in your life, the easier it becomes for you to meet those needs in the future, and the higher your overall quality of life becomes. When you spend your time and energy (and money!) shopping around for "the perfect job" or "the ideal mate," you don't get that benefit.

HOW DO YOU KNOW
WHEN YOU'RE "THERE"?

Because our society is so goal-oriented, people often look at life as a series of goals. It is tempting to view your own path of personal growth as having a goal—perhaps "becoming enlightened," "solving all my problems," or "gaining mastery of life." That is a trap.

Often, when people have their first awakening to their life purpose—when they take their first step on the path of personal growth—they are so overwhelmed with the feelings of delight, power, and meaning that they forget about their commitment to purpose and instead devote themselves to trying to recapture that feeling. Sometimes people are so taken with the incredible value they get from their first encounter with personal growth that they conclude personal growth *is* the purpose of life!

It isn't! At least, it's not the purpose of *my* life, even though writing a book about it happens to be a terrific means for me to fill *my* core needs. If anything, "personal growth" is a strategy for becoming more efficient at living your purpose. Always remember your purpose.

So when have you had enough personal growth that you can start living your life? That's easy: right now. If you're with me this far—if you are clear about your Success Checklist and your purpose statement—you're enlightened enough already. Priority one has to be living your purpose. The personal growth comes from your increased understanding, your creation of new means and structures to fulfill you purpose, and your increased confidence, self-esteem, and self-acceptance as you add up the days, months, and years of living life to the fullest.

20

◆

Resolving Conflicts

*The task of leadership, the first task of concerned people, is
not to condemn or castigate or deplore; it is to search out
the reason for disillusionment and alienation, the rationale
of protest and dissent—perhaps, indeed, to learn from it.*
—Robert F. Kennedy

If you plan to live up to your commitment to have a fantastic life,
you're going to need to stand up for yourself when conflicts occur.
You can be ineffective at resolving conflicts, weather the resulting
storms, and still be committed to your purpose—the commitment is
the most important thing—but there are some skills you can learn
that make handling conflict a whole lot easier.

185

One thing I do, when I'm not writing this book, is officiate youth sports. If you're not familiar with the sport of baseball, I'll explain two points briefly:

First, the sport involves a player called the "pitcher," generally one of the strongest and most talented athletes on a high-school team, throwing a hard ball as fast and hard as he can. He tries to get it past the "batter," who stands 60.5 feet away a with yard-long metal bat weighing about two pounds, swinging as hard as he can. If the batter does not hit the ball, as is often the case, then the "catcher," who kneels right behind the batter, his head just out of range of the swinging bat, attempts to catch the ball, which on a good day comes in at about 80 miles per hour, in a heavily padded leather mitt.

Second, the umpire stands directly behind the catcher, making sure his vision is not blocked by the catcher's head or body. Now, we do wear a mask and some padding, but getting hit in the mask or padding with an 80-mph fast ball still feels like getting hit with an 80-mph fast ball. While the risk of severe bodily harm may be lessened somewhat, it's not an exaggeration to say that, to a certain degree, the quality of my experience as an umpire on any given day depends upon the goodwill of the catcher.

It was through sports officiating that I first learned the value of *rapport*.

RAPPORT

Rapport, essentially, is mutual understanding with a little trust and goodwill thrown in. When Dale Carnegie wrote his famous book *How to Win Friends and Influence People,* he was writing about rapport. It's hard to improve on his suggestions:

- Smile.
- Listen.
- Let people know, genuinely, sincerely, and heartily, the specific things you admire and appreciate about them.

The praise and approval you give people really must be sincere. In order to have rapport with someone, not only do you have to value something about being in their company, but *they have to know it!* Before I understood about rapport, I often jumped right from deciding that I liked someone to teasing and joking around with them, before I did anything to let them know I liked them. Although I teased and joked with genuinely friendly intentions, I had no rapport with them, and they were often puzzled, annoyed, or intimidated. I don't know how many times I got the feedback, "You know, Richard, I really didn't like you at first, but now that I've gotten to know you—" Think of all the people who didn't stick around to get to know me!

Rapport is another one of those things they don't teach you in school. It's like some secret discipline that "popular" people know about and the rest of us don't even know exists. I used to tell jokes that no one would laugh at, even though I had heard someone else tell them the day before and crack everybody up. I couldn't figure out what was wrong with the way I was telling the jokes. Nothing was wrong! I had no rapport—people weren't on my side, didn't want to play along with me, maybe even were looking for a way to knock me down a peg—so they didn't laugh.

RAPPORT AND CONFLICT

When I first started umpiring baseball, I thought the most important thing was knowing the rules. I memorized the rule book; I quizzed myself; I even went to a professional umpire school in Florida for five weeks—the same place the major-league umpires go. By my second season, with my computer-programmer's mind, I probably knew the rules as well as anyone in the world. I kept my uniform neat and clean; I knew where to position myself to get good angles on plays; and my judgment wasn't even that bad. But that season, I ejected 16 coaches and players from games for arguing or protesting decisions I had made.

Now, an umpire has ultimate power in a baseball game. On any play involving judgment, an umpire's decision is final. So I had no need to be defensive, or to argue my position. Working to gain rapport would have worked a lot better than trying to prove I was right. If I had listened to the coach's point of view, let him know I understood it, and left it at that, I could have avoided the escalation that caused at least half of those ejections.

While I hope that any sports officials reading this will find my experience valuable, the main point is this works in real-life relationships as well as baseball relationships. Have you ever had an argument escalate to the point where one of you "ejects" the other? That is an indication you may not have rapport, at least around that subject. Even the best of friends may not have rapport on a particular subject if they don't believe the other really wants to resolve the conflict to mutual satisfaction. The first step in resolving a conflict is to have mutual rapport. Be honest about your genuine

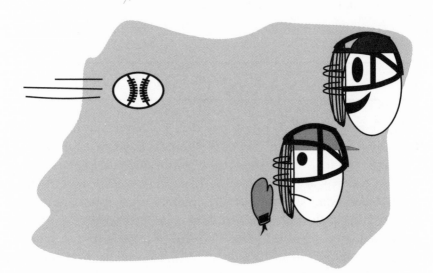

"You know — I really understand your point of view about that last pitch."

desire to find a solution that works for both of you, and ask the other to agree to do the same.

LISTENING

Once both parties are committed to resolving the conflict, the next step is to understand each other's point of view. I used to skip over this step and go straight to proving that I was right, listing all my supporting evidence, and threatening dire consequences if they didn't come around to my point of view.

Don't skip over this step.

The most common trap people fall into, even if they're not as invested in proving they're right as I once was, is skipping over the most important part of the conflict-resolution process: listening to each other's point of view.

> Don't start solving the problem until you know what the problem is!

You may not even be arguing about the same problem. Or even worse, you may both be arguing for the same solution but, since you didn't take time to hear each other's point of view, never realize you are actually in violent agreement. How embarrassing.

What works best, especially if the conflict gets heated, is for one party—that would be you, since you've read the book—to focus exclusively on asking what the other's point of view is, then restating it back, until the other party says, "Yes! That's *exactly* what I mean." At that point, you are free to communicate your own point of view until you're satisfied that the other party understands you.

The great part about this is it works even if *only one of you* is focused on mutual understanding. It takes two to argue, and if just one of you keeps going back to a sincere desire to understand each other's point of view, you'll eventually understand each other.

RESOLUTION

Once you're sure you understand each other's point of view, the resolution to the conflict often comes so quickly that it's anticlimactic. In many cases, the only real problem *was* the lack of understanding, and that's been solved.

Where a difference of opinion remains, however, you'll still want to come to some sort of resolution. But remember the ground rules going into this: both of you have a sincere desire to resolve the conflict to your mutual satisfaction. You really have to believe that for this to work.

> Mutual satisfaction means you're both willing to accept any solution that works for you, even if it means giving up your original point of view.

This is not giving in—this is just acknowledging you're willing to let go of your position if something else acceptable comes along. You may know, deep in your heart and beyond any question, that your original position is the only possible solution that will work for you. That's fine; it doesn't weaken your position at all to say that you'll be open to something you haven't thought of yet—you still get to decide if it's OK with you. And who knows? Something even better than your original position might come along, and if you're not open to alternatives, you've painted yourself into a corner.

You might resolve the conflict by one of you agreeing to the other's point of view, or you might come up with a third proposal that's acceptable to both of you. It's also possible that after you understand each other's position, you'll decide it's not such a big deal after all, and just live with the fact that you disagree on the issue.

WIN/WIN

Naturally, the most attractive solution for you, at least initially, will be your original point of view. That's because you're already clear on the value of that proposal to you—it's what you wanted in the first place.

The problem is, your partner in this conflict does not seem to be clear about the value of your proposal for him or her. Since you have agreed to resolve the conflict to mutual satisfaction, if you want your partner to agree to your proposal, your task is now to find your partner's "win" in it. Because unless there is a win for both of you in the resolution to the conflict, it's not really resolved. Oh, one of you may cave in and decide it's not worth the fight—but the conflict isn't resolved, and it'll probably come up again, and even more heated ("this is the *third time* you've pulled this . . .").

> Any real resolution to a conflict, short of killing one of the parties, is always win/win.

Once you get good at finding the win for other people and letting them know about it, you'll realize you don't even need a conflict! The most successful people are always looking for ways to find the win for other people in what they're doing. Not only do they succeed because they enlist others in their cause, but they pretty quickly get a reputation as someone good to be around—someone who creates opportunities.

This is not "buying favors"—quite the contrary. This is being clear about your purpose and finding ways to create value in line with other people's purposes. It's the most powerful strategy I know for success, and it makes you a nice person to hang out with, too. There are more than five billion people on this planet, and you can get a lot more done together than you can by yourself. And that applies whether we're talking about a CEO and the firm's most junior employee, or you and your Big, Meaningful Relationship.

191

21

◆

Big, Meaningful
Relationships

By all means marry. If you get a good wife, you'll become happy; if you get a bad one, you'll become a philosopher.
— *Socrates*

How am I going to cover the subject of relationships in one short chapter when entire libraries have been written on the subject and it's still not clear humanity has made any progress? Well, let's give it a shot. To save space, I'm going to limit my discussion to relationships that *work*. If you want to learn the attitudes and behavior patterns necessary to have relationships that *don't* work, you can get them from most TV shows.

Let's start with the romantic model of relationships. A young lady—let's call her Julie—gets dragged to this party her parents are throwing for their friends, including this scary dude her mom wants to fix her up with. Not being particularly attracted to him, she spends most of the evening hiding behind the drapes, wondering if there's something wrong with her for not being interested in this guy her parents are so fond of.

Meanwhile, a young man—let's call him Roman—crashes the party on a dare from some of his friends. His family wasn't invited because of his dad's politics. So, not wanting the hosts to spot him and not having much else to do there, he also hangs out behind the drapes.

Call it Fate. Kismet. The Stars. Whatever. They meet. In one passionate glance, they know they are soulmates. Finally, at long last, their lives of despair are over, for they have met the one who will fulfill their destiny, satisfy their yearnings, and make them happy forever. Ahh. Ain't love grand?

So what happens next?

From the standpoint of love and attraction, they're off to a great start, aren't they? But if they want to live happily ever after— well, they've got some work to do. No relationship, even with the most wonderful person you've ever imagined, is going to automatically "fulfill your destiny," "satisfy your yearnings," or "make you happy" indefinitely without a lot of work on your part. However, if you're willing to do the work, a Big, Meaningful Relationship can be a great investment. Plus, you get to be in love. Sigh.

A FULFILLING RELATIONSHIP

Now that you have your Success Checklist, having a great relationship is a straightforward process. Just as in any other part of your life, you can find the missing core needs by ticking down your Checklist, then use one of the methods on page 182 to find ways to fill them constructively.

I want to bring in the concept of accountability here, just to stress that your power to have a great relationship is largely determined by how you view the relationship. If you look at your relationship from the victim point of view, you'll see it as something that *happens to you*.

> If you expect any of your core needs to be filled by your mate, rather than take responsibility for filling them yourself, you're a relationship victim.

That's not to say your mate *won't* act in ways that help you fill your core needs; I'm just saying it's not *primarily* his or her job to create the means and structures that fulfill *your* needs: it's yours. If you and your mate are both clear about your Success Checklists, I think it would be a wonderful thing to brainstorm together about things to do, ways to live, or commitments to make together that would fill core needs for both of you. But it's not a *requirement*.

If you take the accountable point of view in your relationship, you'll realize the choices you make determine whether your needs get met constructively. If you're missing some core needs in your relationship, make some different choices. These new choices could include being more assertive about what you want in the relationship; coming up with new things to do together that are more fulfilling for you; spending more time doing activities that don't involve your mate; or simply changing your point of view about something.

There is such an abundance of ways to get each core need met that there's always something else to try. As long as the two of you want to stay together—and if you have made a lifelong commitment, that's till death do you part—you will always be able to come up with a new idea for a way to meet one of your neglected core needs. If you feel like saying, "I've tried everything," add "I've tried everything" to your list of excuses, and try again. You haven't. You could live a billion years and still not try everything.

It's even possible to have a great relationship if your mate hasn't read this book! It only takes one person to be accountable. And filling your own needs will make you a more enjoyable person for your partner, and everyone, for that matter, to be around. If you want the relationship to work, you've got to take charge of filling your Success Checklist.

LEADING BY EXAMPLE

At this point, some of you may be asking what the point is of having a relationship at all if you're just going to have to meet all your needs yourself. I'm not saying you have to make the other person unnecessary! I'm just suggesting the best way to get all the items on your Success Checklist filled constructively is to be accountable, rather than depending on someone else. And if you're really invested in getting one or more of your needs met *by the other person*, I recommend leading by example.

I always thought the Golden Rule—"do unto others as you would have them do unto you"—was something people were "supposed to" follow just because "good people" followed it. I thought it was some moral code, to be adhered to out of a sense of justice and fair play. But the Golden Rule is more than that—it's the simplest, most effective strategy I know for meeting your core needs. If one of your core needs is "respect," be respectful with your mate. If your core need for "beauty" is missing from your relationship, take steps to be more beautiful or create more beauty yourself.

Lead by example! When you do, two things happen. First, if you're really doing these things just because you want to, and not to try to manipulate or induce guilt in your mate, chances are they will learn from the example you're setting and eventually start to give back some of the experiences you've been creating yourself. Second, you may be surprised to learn it works just as well for you to create those experiences yourself as it would for your mate to create them for you.

> Your sense of fulfillment comes from meeting all the
> items on your Success Checklist—and it doesn't make
> a difference in the quality of your life whether it's
> you, your mate, or someone else who's setting up the
> structure to meet them.

Playing by the Golden Rule, or simply being the way you want others to be, works in any relationship. In fact, you may find as a result of treating other people the way you want to be treated you start attracting new friends into your life who want to treat you the same way back.

COMMUNICATION AGAIN

Suppose one of Fred's core needs is "feeling special." Yet Fred's wife Trudy doesn't do all the little things for him that make him feel special—you know, the things his mother did for him, like bring him a cup of warm chocolate milk in the morning, or cut his peanut-butter sandwiches into triangles. Fred feels bad because he wants Trudy to make him feel special, and she doesn't. What can Fred do?

First of all, this idea of "making him feel" special is a trap. That kind of phrasing leads to looking at the situation from a victim point of view: Trudy may behave in a certain way, and Fred may feel a certain way when he's around her, but it's Fred who's making Fred feel how Fred feels.

So Fred, being an enlightened husband and being accountable for his own fulfillment, decides to lead by example. Every morning, he goes downstairs and microwaves two glasses of chocolate milk—one for each lovebird. And he starts making bag lunches for Trudy to take with her to her job as a US Senator—each peanut-butter sandwich cut into little triangles. Although Trudy seems puzzled, and doesn't respond favorably at first, Fred knows leading by

197

example takes time, and he keeps giving away what he wants, unselfishly, for as long as it takes.

And in fact, Fred feels better already, because he discovers that his giving Trudy special treatment helps meet *his own* core need to feel special. Then, one day, as Fred is treating Trudy especially special—in addition to the warm chocolate milk and the peanut-butter triangles, he lays out her pajamas for her at night—Trudy blows up. "*When* are you going to stop treating me like a *child?*" she exclaims. "I'm a US Senator! Haven't I earned the right to a little respect?"

Poor Fred. What we have here is a failure to communicate.

Remember from Chapter 18 that the same activity or experience can fill very different core needs for different people? While Fred considered warm chocolate milk, triangular sandwiches, and laid-out pajamas to be special treatment, Trudy considered the same things to be disrespectful, or treating her like a child. Although Fred's intention was to give Trudy special treatment, that's not what she received.

Whose fault was it? It doesn't matter. But since Fred is accountable, he is willing to take the steps necessary to iron out this miscommunication. He apologizes to Trudy, since it wasn't his intention at all to show disrespect. He wanted her to feel special. He asks her what he could do that would make her feel special. Trudy thinks a while, then says, "Actually, now that I understand your intentions, I kind of like your bringing up breakfast. But could you make mine orange juice? Cold orange juice?"

Fred beams. "Sure! Anything else?"

Trudy replies, "Well, I didn't want to mention this, because I thought you'd think I had a swelled head, but if you really want me to feel special, when you introduce me to your friends, I'd really like it if you referred to me as 'Senator' rather than 'the little lady.' "

"Really?" Fred says. "Gosh—I always called you 'the little lady' because I wanted you to feel special."

With the misunderstanding ironed out, things go a lot smoother in the Fred and Trudy household. Trudy never does come around to bringing Fred breakfast or making lunch for him, but Fred is surprised to discover it's not such a big deal any more. In fact, in addition to the satisfaction he gets simply by *giving her* special treatment, the increased intimacy in their relationship as a result of understanding each other's needs better makes Fred feel very special.

With much continued hard work, which is well worth it, they live happily ever after.

22

◆

Pitfalls

I cannot give you the formula for success, but I can give you the formula for failure—which is: Try to please every-body.

—Herbert B. Swope

It's easy to focus on one thing—for instance, on filling your Success Checklist—and ignore the other things you need to do to have a great life—for instance, taking care of those undones and honoring your commitments. So this chapter is a kind of "troubleshooting guide," like at the back of the VCR instructions where it says, "If pressing the POWER button does not turn on the VCR, check to see if it's plugged in." If you get stuck on your road to happiness, flip back to this chapter and see if you've fallen into any of these pitfalls.

USE FULFILLMENT STRATEGIES, NOT SURVIVAL STRATEGIES

If there's only one piece of bread on the table, and you're starving, it makes sense to do whatever it takes to get that bread. You'll guard it jealously, grab for it quickly, and be wary of other people who may lie, cheat, or steal to get it. That piece of bread is a matter of survival: whoever gets it wins, and the others lose. In a world of scarcity, survival is a win/lose game.

However, quality of life is not scarce. If I have a great life, that doesn't keep anyone else from having one too—in fact, I would argue that the more happy, fulfilled people there are walking around, the easier it is for everyone to have a great life. People who are enjoying life are fun to be around, great to learn from, and naturally contribute to the lives of those around them. Fulfillment is a realm of abundance, not scarcity, and the best strategies for fulfillment are based on win/win, not win/lose.

Some of the strategies people use in a win/lose game are distrust, secrecy, trickery, manipulation, and hoarding. If you play life as a win/lose game, two things can happen: if you're good at it, you'll end up making a lot of enemies and alienating people who are win/win players; or if you're not so good at it, you'll simply end up without much to show for yourself. Of course, you may get a certain level of fulfillment out of playing the game, but you could probably get just as much out of playing a win/win game—and have all those potential enemies be on your side instead!

If you notice yourself playing win/lose in an area of your life that isn't working so well, the game you're playing may be the reason. All the energy you put into keeping other people down is wasted energy that you could be using to have a great life. And win/lose players attract other win/lose players, so if you get really good at it, you have the reward of hanging out with a bunch of distrustful, secretive, manipulative, hoarding tricksters. What fun.

The concept behind win/win is extremely simple: all the players look for opportunities to help each other in ways that bear little cost to themselves. Instead of just thinking, "What's in it for me?" the win/win player also thinks, "What's in it for you?" It's like you and I are assembling jigsaw puzzles, and I notice I have the missing piece to your puzzle. Giving you the piece to your puzzle costs me nothing, and helps you out. Do I demand, or expect, that you give me a piece of my puzzle before I give you yours? No! Who cares? I'm doing it because I believe in win/win.

Even if I know I'm never going to see you again, and you'll never have a chance to help me out, I'm still going to do it. Why not? It didn't cost me much, and I know playing win/win in general is the best strategy for having a great life. Just as win/lose players attract other win/lose players, win/win attracts win/win. Those are the kind of people I want to hang out with.

If survival isn't hanging in the balance, make sure the game you're playing is a win/win fulfillment game, not a win/lose survival game.

GET OUT OF YOUR COMFORT ZONE

The main reason people don't *instantly* transform their lives from OK to WOW! usually has to do with their "comfort zone." Change—even constructive change—causes discomfort. I remember trading in a clunker of a car I owned—a car that gave me nothing but problems the whole time I owned it—for a beautiful, brand-new sports car. Although the new car was better in every way, the first few times I drove it, I was distinctly uncomfortable every time I put my foot on the clutch—just because it felt different from the old clunker.

Discomfort simply comes from change—it doesn't mean things are getting worse, just different! The more temporary discomfort you're willing to put up with, the quicker you can add more fulfillment to your life. Fulfillment feels good a lot more than discomfort feels bad!

Fear is another temporary symptom of getting out of your comfort zone. Unless the fear is related to physical danger, it's not a sound basis for making decisions. The fear is your unconscious telling you some similar situation in the past was scary or dangerous. Well, it's not the past any more, and if you're clear about the value of what you're doing, you can ignore the fear. Notice it—and do it anyway.

If the changes you're making honor your commitments and help you fill your Success Checklist constructively, you're on the right track. You're out of your comfort zone—but out of it on the right side, past OK! That discomfort means you've broken free into new levels of fulfillment, and it just feels different. You're in great shape! Don't change back!

QUESTION YOUR ASSUMPTIONS

If some area of your life isn't working well, check out your assumptions. Are there things you feel like you *can't* or *have to* do? Remember, most "can't's" and all "have to's" are really a choice—think about what the alternatives would be if you *did* take the afternoon off, or you *didn't* agree to pick her up at the airport. I've found some of the things I felt I just couldn't do were based, deep down, on some silly belief I got programmed with when I was seven. Question those beliefs, and see if they're working for you!

Some beliefs, like those that start with "I can't," seem true, but are really self-fulfilling prophecies. If you strengthen the belief that you *are able*, rather than that you *can't*, you can turn those prophecies around. It's better to increase your chances of success by betting on yourself, even if you risk feeling bad if you fail, than to expect failure and thereby make failure more likely.

Without consciously choosing your beliefs, you'll end up with whatever your head happened to get filled up with as you grew up. That may not bear any relationship to the truth, to what works best for you, or to what would support you in living your life purpose. It's so easy for catchy beliefs to spread, even if they're utterly false. Don't be a human chain letter—you've got to rely on yourself!

BE NICE TO YOURSELF

Many of us have grown up being motivated by criticism. It really is motivating—but commitment to purpose is even more motivating. None of the great heroes of history ever got books written about them because they did something they had to do to avoid being punished!

If you're someone who tends to be hard on yourself, please try a different way. Still do your best, but when you stumble, pat yourself on the back for striving hard enough to risk failure. Build yourself up, rather than cut yourself down, and you'll be in better shape to live your purpose. Learn from your mistakes; don't kill yourself with them.

RISK OTHER PEOPLE'S DISAPPROVAL

The toughest part of living up to my commitment to have a great life was when I risked losing other people's approval. I was reluctant to suggest changes in my job responsibilities because I thought my boss and coworkers would disapprove. I was reluctant to ask for what I wanted in relationships because I was afraid people would reject me or think I had no right to ask. Since growing up, for me, was all about learning how to get other people's approval, it was way out of my comfort zone to risk losing it.

Bit by bit, though, I gritted my teeth and remembered that my commitment to my purpose in life was more important than giving in to my fear. I already knew what it felt like to live for external approval, and I wasn't willing to go back to that. So I asked anyway.

It was rarely as difficult as I had imagined, and most of the time it was far easier. I was constantly amazed at how willing people were to adapt to me! And I get more approval, by far, now that I live life with a clear commitment to my purpose than I did when I was uncertain and hungry for approval.

The nice thing is, the more you honor your commitments to yourself, the more you approve of yourself, and *the less approval from others you need.* It's as if you need a certain amount of approval to feel OK, and if you get it from yourself by living a life of purpose, meaning, and integrity, you don't need as much from other people. If you sell yourself short, sacrificing your own life purpose to get external approval, you just create a need for even more approval from others, because you've betrayed yourself.

Maybe the best way to look at it is this: if those people really care about you, then they'll want you to have a great life. And if they don't—why on earth would you care about getting their approval? Be true to yourself.

FINISH WHAT YOU START

Keep that to-do list short! It eats up energy and feels awful. If it's getting too long, get out your date book and schedule all your undones for specific dates and times. Maintaining a constant state of crisis takes so much energy that there's not much left for the good stuff!

LEARN FROM GUILT, RESENTMENT, AND SELF-PITY

Guilt is a signal you're not accepting yourself. Resentment is a signal you're not accepting the way someone else is. Self-pity is a signal you're not accepting that what happened happened. What is is. What was was. Find the reality you're denying. Once you accept reality, then if you still want to you can work for change. Acceptance is the most powerful first step for change.

BE HUNGRY FOR FEEDBACK

Feedback from other people is often free, and is the most valuable source of information about yourself outside yourself. Welcome it, rather than resist it. Your great opportunities for growth come from the times when you think everything's going great, and you get the rug pulled out from under you. Get as much feedback as you can.

While hearing negative feedback is often painful, consider the alternative—you could be like the emperor in his "new clothes," walking around naked until someone was brave enough to give him feedback. If you suspect things are going awry—if you sense someone is upset, or resenting you—ask sincerely for feedback. Then listen, listen, listen until *they are satisfied* you heard what they had to say.

Genuinely work to understand other people's point of view. If someone else thinks something is important, and you don't understand why, congratulations! You have found an opportunity to learn and grow. And believe me, as soon as you really understand what's going on, five other people will crawl out of the woodwork who had the same issue with you, but weren't willing to confront you. It's worth it.

BE TRUE TO YOURSELF

Every time you break an agreement with yourself, every time you violate a structure you have chosen to honor in your life, every time you abandon a commitment you have made, you hurt yourself. And you know what? Most likely, no one will ever catch you, no one will confront you, you'll never have to pay for it except in the most direct way: you'll have a worse life.

When you undermine yourself by weakening your integrity, you instantly lower your quality of life. That's what people mean when they say, "Virtue is its own reward." Do whatever it takes to live your life purpose within your commitments, and be true to yourself.

23

◆

Happily Ever After

*To burn always with this hard, gemlike flame, to maintain
this ecstasy, is success in life.*

— Walter Pater

If you're feeling a little panicky because this book is almost over
and you're not past OK yet, stay calm. You can have the blueprint
for a house in your hands, and all the building materials delivered to
your lot, and not have a house yet. This stuff really works, but only if
you actually do it. The speed with which you make progress in your
life is completely up to you.

If you have read the book but didn't do any of the written exercises, why not go back and really do them? In writing. Your reasons for not doing them in writing would be a great start for your Excuses list—you probably use the same excuses for all sorts of things. If you've given 100% and done all the written exercises, you're in great shape—the next step is to put your plans into action.

Doing that will have three parts, which correspond roughly to the three parts of this book:

- *Understanding* life and how the world works. You'll get the maximum benefit by seizing every opportunity to learn about things you don't understand, rather than using lack of understanding as an excuse to shut things out of your life.

- *Accepting* yourself, other people, and the world as they currently are—you can still want change, but it works best to accept first, and change second. Energy spent on guilt, resentment, and self-pity is wasted energy that you could spend instead on having a great life.

- *Committing* to honor what is most important to you, and make choices in alignment with that, rather than inertia, fear, or other people's approval. That means setting up structures in your life that support your Success Checklist, and honoring the structures you have chosen.

People who don't get past OK get stuck in one of these three places. How about you?

Have you stopped learning? Have you caught yourself in a Truth Trap of beliefs so strong there's no room for new ways of looking at life? Or do you look at every attitude you don't understand as a learning opportunity, every disagreement as a chance to understand a new point of view? If you don't understand how someone could disagree with you, but they do, there's a good chance doing the work to understand their point of view will help propel you on your way to a higher quality of life.

Are you holding your breath waiting for change—from your mate, the world, or even yourself? It's fine to *want* change, but please accept the way things are now and go right ahead with your purpose in life *based on today's reality.*

Is the idea of having a fantastic life just a nice fantasy bubble that bursts when life's slings and arrows come your way? Or are you *committed* to get past OK? Have you made the decision to have your life mean something—to spend it on what matters most to you?

THE LAST WORD ON PURPOSE

The moral of this story, I suppose, is that as long as you're alive, you might as well have the best life you can. People feel most alive when they are committed to some purpose and doing all they can to fulfill it. That's why people often reminisce about their college days, or their days fighting a war. For that period of time, they felt alive with purpose.

Many organizations get people to serve their own agendas by indoctrinating them with a sense of purpose. From religious cults to corporations, people value that sense of purpose so much they are willing to sacrifice their own personal fulfillment to become part of a group that gives the appearance of doing something important. And people who've been that route and been burned often shy away from the whole idea of purpose.

I am convinced living a life of purpose feels better for you, and results in more approval from other people, than the alternative. So the question becomes, what purpose should you choose? By choosing your own unique purpose that incorporates all the items on your Success Checklist, you'll have something that you can stick to your whole life, that you can always fulfill in some way or another, and that touches everything in your life that you find meaningful, worthwhile, or just plain fun. What else is there to do?

ON YOUR OWN?

I'll end this book where I started it, by talking about self-reliance. If you've made the choice to be the final authority on what's right for you—and I sincerely hope you have—you may notice some new feelings and perspectives on life. You may experience some discomfort—perhaps a sense of going it alone.

In one sense, if you've committed to self-reliance, you really are on your own now. Gone forever is the womb-like comfort of believing there's some person, organization, or book out there that can reassure you you're living life "right." Leaving the womb is the price we pay for the privilege of living.

But in another sense, you're not alone at all. There are lots of us out here who have made the same commitment—to be the final authority on our own lives, to give up childhood, to stop the buck with us. Welcome! I suggest you surround yourself as much as possible with people who are committed to living life to the fullest. Get to know them. I was surprised, and delighted, to learn that many, many of those people consider helping others to be a main part of their own life purpose. I was even more surprised when I discovered I was one of those people! So this book is my best shot, to date, at helping people make progress in their lives. I hope you've found it to be the most important thing you've ever read—or at least laughed at a few of my jokes.

Whatever you choose to do from this moment forward, make it mean something to you. And have a fantastic life!

Your next steps in personal growth may include:

- ☑ books
- ☑ workshops and seminars
- ☑ audio cassettes
- ☑ computer software

Please write or call for our free catalog
using the coupon at the back of this book.

ACKNOWLEDGMENTS

Thank you for reading my book.

My wife and best friend, Dana Brodie, encouraged and supported me to start, continue, and finish this book. She helped me formulate many ideas, and contributed a great deal to my enjoyment of the writing process.

Bill Bader and Matt Senft supported me for months with their inextinguishable excitement about the project. Both read enough versions of the manuscript to make their eyes blur.

Cathy Habib, Dave Kaplan, Greg Kusnick, Steve Salta, and Paul Vick reviewed drafts of the book with great thoroughness and enthusiasm, and all provided particularly valuable suggestions for improvements. I am particularly indebted to Greg Kusnick for pointing out that pot roast is not cooked in an oven.

Bill Gates, Steve Hazlerig, Mike Koss, George Lynn, Suchada MacDonald, Mike Mee, Dave Moore, Gudrun Niosi, Randy Revell, Charles Simonyi, and Melissa Stewart also took a significant amount of time out of their schedules to review drafts and give me feedback.

Martha Salta kindly gave me several creative and helpful suggestions for the illustrations.

Java Joe kept me well lubricated with double tall nonfat *ristretto* lattes throughout this entire process, for which I am eternally grateful.

Context Associated's well-crafted Excellence Series of seminars introduced me to many of the ideas in this book, not to mention my wife.

And to everyone else who, when you found out I was writing a book, responded with enthusiasm and encouragement rather than skepticism—thanks.

INDEX

B

C

F

G

H

I

M

Q

R

Order Form

☎ **Telephone Orders:**   Call toll-free 1-800-PAST-OK-1. Please
                          have your Visa or MasterCard ready.

💻 **Fax Orders:**   (206) 727-5130.

✉ **Mail Orders:**   Integral Press
                         1202 East Pike Street, Suite 786-B
                         Seattle, WA 98122-3934
                         (206) 328-2217

☐ Please send _____ copies of GETTING PAST OK ($9.95 each)
☐ Please send free catalog of books, audio, and software.
☐ Please send free information about seminars and workshops.

—Satisfaction Guaranteed—
You may return your purchase at any time for a full refund.

Name: _____

Address: _____

_____

City: _____ State: _____ Zip: _____ - ___

Sales Tax: Please add 8.2% for orders shipped to Washington State.

Shipping:

☐Book rate: $2.00 for the first book plus 75¢ for each additional
         book. (Allow three to four weeks for surface shipping.)
☐Air mail: $3.50 per book.

Payment: ☐ Check   ☐ Visa ☐ MasterCard

Card number:_____

Name on card: _____ Exp. date: ___ / ___